T

The Forgotten People

Tony Williams

First Impression—1997

ISBN 1 85902 462 9

© Tony Williams

Printed in Wales at
Gomer Press, Llandysul, Ceredigion

For the people of the
Fort Berthold Reservation

Contents

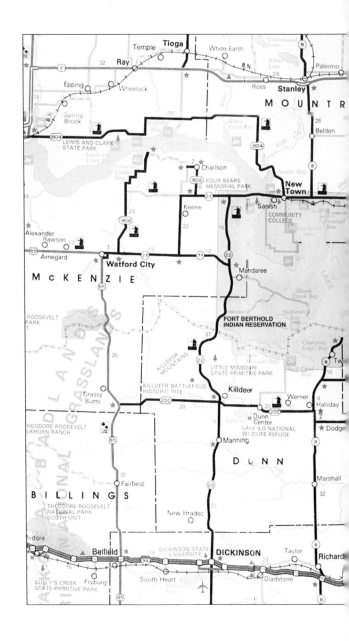

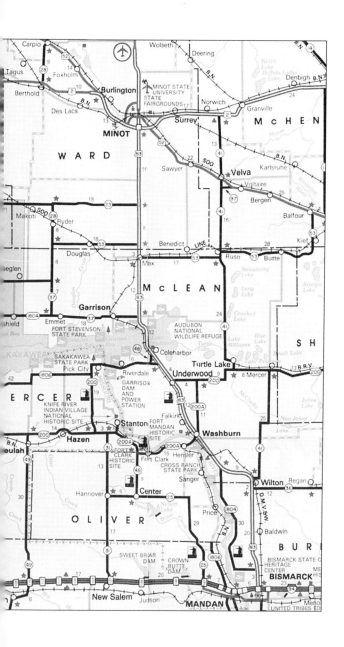

Prologue

Surrounded by greenery, birdsong and the sounds of lapping water, Harry Sitting Bear floated in his little tub down the River Teifi in West Wales.

The foliage was rich, and this powerfully built American Indian was in a small craft made of willow and calico. It was a Welsh coracle. His own people made coracles, too, but they called them bull boats.

We were walking along the bank, Cathy and I, glimpsing Harry through gaps in the greenery. Another eye watched him, too, the electronic eye of a film camera, capturing his short journey along this stretch of the river at Cilgerran Gorge.

In another coracle, engaged in animated conversation with the big Native American, was Bernard Thomas, a 74-year-old craftsman who is one of the last of his kind. He makes coracles, by hand, just a few miles away from where we were filming.

In their different ways, these two men are trying to preserve bits of history. Bernard Thomas wants to keep alive a skill that is dying. Harry Sitting Bear was here, having been sent by his tribal elders, to pursue the possible link between his people and mine. Both were being filmed by a documentary maker and my hope is that this book and that film will put an old debate back on the agenda.

In the late eighteenth century a ruler of the Cherokee nation called Chief Oconostota talked of white people who had crossed the great water many, many years ago.

Harry Sitting Bear and Bernard Thomas on the Teifi.

His grandfather had told him they were a people called the Welsh. Oconstota is mentioned in a letter written by Governor John Sevier of Tennessee in October 1810. Sevier says he had discovered a very ancient fortification, and mentioned this to Oconostota. The old chief said that, according to stories handed down by his forefathers, such fortifications had been made by white people, who had come to the country many years before.

He said the white people and the Cherokee had fought over several years. On one occasion, the Cherokee saw the white people making boats, and supposed they were going down the Tennessee River. There was more combat. Then there was a truce. The whites said they would leave the Cherokee country if there could be an end to hostilities and an exchange of prisoners. This was agreed.

The whites are said to have travelled down the Tennessee River to Ohio, then down the Mississippi, and then to have branched off into its large tributary, the Missouri.

It was when Sevier asked Oconostota who these white people were that the old chief said he had heard his grandfather say they were the Welsh, a people who had reached this land many years before, and had landed at what we now know as Mobile Bay in Alabama.

Harry Sitting Bear is not Cherokee. Harry is Mandan. The Mandan Indians are physiognomically different in several ways from other tribes—fairer of hair, fairer of skin. There are also linguistic differences between them and the Sioux, from whose stock they may have come. Other similarities will become apparent as I tell here of my attempts to reopen what is an old debate. Although I instinctively believe old Oconstota's story, there are others who are far more sceptical. On the journeys that I made to north America with my wife, Cathy, and our children, and afterwards, in writing this book, I wanted to discover for myself the truth about the Mandans. My aim from the start has been to bring enough new evidence to show that the Mandans are truly related to the Welsh, that they indeed were the descendants of a twelfth-century Welsh prince called Madoc.

Madoc sailed for the New World in 1170, taking some three hundred people with him. He may have sailed in a Viking ship, or a stolen English one.

His people probably merged with the Sioux after several struggles as they ascended through their newfound land. The half-breeds who were the result of this merger then left the Sioux nation and became the Mandan.

Mandan Indians live today on a reservation with two other tribes: the Hidatsa and the Arikara. But only the Mandans have this link with Wales.

Harry Sitting Bear believes he and I may well have ancestors in common. We'll never know, of course. No one will ever know. But there is much evidence that nags and nags and will not go away. There are the boats. There are artefacts whose production is very similar. There are architectural similarities. There are linguistic similarities.

And there are stories. Stories have a habit of not going away, too. While nothing is written to show that Madoc established a colony in the New World three hundred years before Christopher Columbus got there, there is much to suggest he did.

I am not a historian, nor am I an anthropologist. I am a former school caretaker who has an adventurous streak, who wants to discover, to try things for himself, and not sit back and take things for granted. Already I have led my wife and three children to become the 'Swiss Family Williams' by going to a desert island and exposing us all to the mercy of the baking sun and the fates.* We might still be there now had my younger son not become ill.

But destiny steered me back to Wales, and subsequently to the land of the Mandan American Indians. And I'm glad it did, because it sent me on a journey neither I nor Cathy—nor, for that matter, my three children—will ever forget.

What I have attempted to do in this book is put together the story of my stay among the Mandans in North Dakota, of my long conversations with them, of

*Tony Williams, *Island of Dreams*, London, Signet, 1994.

the interest taken in my quest by an English film-maker and the subsequent filming both in the USA and in my native Wales. Occasionally I will turn aside from my story and relate some history, both of the Mandans and of the Welsh.

Our stay with the Mandans—and among those with whom they share the reservation in North Dakota, the Hidatsa and the Arikara—has had a profound effect on me and my family. While the possibility of a link between the Mandans and a seafaring prince from north Wales has been dismissed before, there are still a lot of people on both sides of the Atlantic who believe it is there. If this book manages to reopen the argument between scholars and possibly establish some twinning arrangements between Welsh towns and those on the Forth Berthold reservation, then I feel it will have done its job.

Part one:

The Bad Lands of Dakota

Chapter One

A journey postponed

It sounds strange to say my story begins more than eight hundred years ago, but that about sums it up. If a certain Welsh prince called Madoc had not set foot—as I believe he did—in America three hundred years before a certain Italian navigator sailed from Spain and did the same, I might never have become the adventurer I am.

For it was Madoc's voyage—and my subsequent researches into it—that set my adventurous spirit on the move again. It has led my family and me to an extraordinary stay among that Native American people, the Mandans. And I hope to show that this line of American Indians came—with some interbreeding along the way—ultimately from north Wales.

Prince Madoc's journey is said to have been in 1170. He and three hundred men set foot in what we now term the New World. I say 'set foot in' rather than 'discovered', because how can you possibly discover something that is already populated? It's a point I usually make to people who say America was 'discovered' by one Cristóbal Colón (1451–1506), more familiar to us as Christopher Columbus.

We had been planning our trip to North Dakota for some time. But bad news came, which changed our plans. We learned of the death of Tapu, wife of William Richard, a school inspector we met while we were seeking our 'island of dreams' in 1993. (Indeed, a book of that same title came out in 1994, telling of our stay on a desert island.) It was on Rarotonga, capital of the Cook Islands, that we had met William and Tapu, before we went one step further in our search for paradise, to the little island of Maina; we had got to know the couple well, found them friendly and helpful beyond measure. And now Tapu was dead and buried, and William's letter, as well as informing us of that, asked us to be at the unveiling of the headstone.

She had been a shy, generous lady who'd made us so welcome. Now we'd never see her again, and naturally we wanted to honour her memory.

So we had to postpone our investigation of the famous Mandan-Madoc link—but at least the trip, sad though its purpose was, afforded us the opportunity to see once more our island of dreams, Maina.

As we travelled, the kids getting restless, Matthew struggling to see *Mr Bean* on the in-flight screen, I could see again those headlines that had captured our first adventure, especially the one in the *Daily Mirror*: 'If this is being a castaway you can shipwreck me any time . . .' That was Harry Arnold, the writer of the article, quoting me. His feature began: 'Dawn breaks in the South Pacific. On a tiny island a deeply tanned man rises from his bed of woven leaves and casts a net into the ocean.'

In a way, our experiences on Maina, a hundred and fifty miles to the southwest of Rarotonga and a mere speck in the oh, so blue ocean, had been a kind of preparation for research into Native American culture.One quest had led naturally to another, and they were certainly not unconnected. Ever since I was a lad I'd longed to be cast away on a desert island, and ever since I was a lad I'd been interested in other peoples, how they lived, how they survived in ways very different from our own. I think it's helpful to say something here about our desert island and my questing spirit—I suppose it helps to put other things about me and my unorthodox family into perspective. Why, for instance, did a former school caretaker from Swansea decide to uproot and take his family to distant parts of the world for the sake of exploration? Most people do that when they want to emigrate or visit relatives or go on a package tour. Not me.

I was thirty-one when we were on Maina in 1993. Craig, our eldest, was eleven, Matthew was seven and Stacey was just four. While we were there we all contributed to our existence. I fished and built our accommodation. Cathy cooked and taught the kids. Craig

The island of Maina

climbed trees for coconuts and fruit, with Matthew helping by collecting up the coconuts Craig had dropped to the ground. He also had the additional task of gathering firewood. And Even Stacey, who seemed to adapt better than any of us, had her jobs to do: as well as helping Matthew with the firewood, she turned out to be the best at picking the fish from the net.

When it was over, and we had to return earlier than expected because of Matthew's illness, I remarked how nice it would be to stay there for ever.

We had survived off the land. We had had to get on well as a family—and did so, discovering that not only was it necessary, not only possible, but pleasurable. With hindsight, we all realize now how such cooperation—rarely seen these days in Western family life—was essential to existence in small communities that relied on the flora and fauna for their day-to-day subsistence.

I think I can trace my own fascination for such things to my younger years when I mixed a lot with the older generations—people who had experienced that greater sense of community and collective existence so necessary to life on a desert island or within a Native American village of old.

I remember listening to the stories of the old school caretaker who'd been a prisoner of war, and who, with his fellow prisoners, had had to work in the copper mines. I remember Gertie Jones, the next-door-neighbour of my teenage years, a woman of great character and humour. She was in her seventies and, if we kids were getting in her hair, she'd bustle us off with the teasing comment, 'Go on boys, go home quickly—your mothers are making plain cakes with currants in . . .' I spent many a day listening to her stories about Swansea in the 1930s—of Woolworth's, say, where everything was sixpence or less.

Now, maturing, I've watched these people pass on, out of my life; but they've left me with a great feeling for community, for living life the way things were. Perhaps it's just a romantic notion that things were better in days gone by. Certainly, there were things that we wouldn't want now: the degree of illness and poverty, for instance, that we don't get in Britain in the nineties—although there's still poverty aplenty.

Perhaps it was that which led me to the desert island of Maina. Perhaps it was also the rebel in me, the part of me that rejected the sort of life I could see eating away at my contemporaries, stuck in their council houses or their semis, drudging away at their existences, knowing, probably, that this would be how they'd live for the rest of their dreary, meaningless lives.

Perhaps it was also the romantic in me, the part of me that had visualized life on a desert island for as long as I could remember. Hardly a day went past in my earlier life when I didn't talk about an island, and I could see warm sand and blue skies and trees dripping with lush coconuts. I suppose I also heard twanging guitars in my mind's ear, too! Ah, the stuff of dreams!

Yet I was certain that I could truly live in such a place someday—with no telephones, no cars, no competition and high-octane living, no fighting with the local council when something went wrong with the house. And if I could, I told myself—if I could just live on that island—I'd be a happy man.

When I was younger I would ask so-called educated people about *The Mutiny on the Bounty* and heroes like

Captain Bligh. I'd ask them whether there were still desert islands in the world. And they'd look away embarrassed and not be able to answer me. Or thought I was being naive or excessively romantic. But I make no apologies for that. Anyway, they had no knowledge of just how little I knew of life outside Britain, away from city life, busy roads, polluted air. I felt there was a great gaping hole in my education, and I wanted to fill it.

I'd been talking about finding a desert island before I'd met Cathy. It was a full ten years before I actually went to one—our 'dummy run', without the kids, on another South Pacific island, four years before our stay on Maina in 1993. So it had been a long time a-coming. But come it did, and I was happy to stick two fingers up to those who had doubted that I'd ever do it, especially the snooty headmaster at a school I worked at who looked down his nose at me and my romantic ideas.

Anyway, it was with no regrets at all that we were returning to the Cook Islands at the end of 1995, happy to be spending Christmas there.

Our ambitions to prove the Mandan-Madoc link had to be temporarily shelved.

Chapter Two

Like minds

I was seventeen when I first met Cathy. She was seventeen, too, and had red hair and a freckled face. We talked all the time of our dreams and interests. I talked to her of books I'd read. *Mutiny on the Bounty* was one that had always captivated me. I told her of the war on Pitcairn Island, which had been inhabited in 1790 by mutineers from HMS *Bounty* and their Tahitian companions, some of whose descendants still live there. I talked of how the mutineers who settled there had fought each other and couldn't live together; yet they couldn't get off the island because they'd burnt their only means of escape: the *Bounty*.

Cathy would listen intently to this romantic talk. But she had a romantic streak, too. Both of us had developed a passion for the Brontës—particularly Emily Brontë, and her *Wuthering Heights*. We often referred to our little Stacy as 'our Brontë girl', because she was conceived while Cathy and I were on a trip to Haworth Vicarage, the Brontë family home.

The whole village was filled with the spirit of the nineteenth century—or at least, I suppose, a romantic idealization of it, for you can never really recapture what's gone. But there it was, with its small shops and cobbled streets, and it certainly appealed to the romantic in *me*.

The other passion that began to grow in Cathy and in me was one which had lain slumbering since my childhood and was rekindled in me as we browsed through some old books in Swansea central library after our return from the South Pacific. This was a fascination for the lives and ways of American Indians. Now there was someone I could talk to about it.

The word 'Indian' is a misnomer, of course. It comes from Columbus's belief that he'd found a new route to India. But the name was kept, and the word 'American' was added. Subsequently, as we know, many people call them Native Americans, although some natives retain the word 'Indian' when describing themselves.

These peoples came from Asia across the Bering Straits more than twenty thousand years ago during the last Ice Age. Perhaps I ought to say *most* of them did, because my interest is in one particular people, the Mandans, and how I believe they were descended from Prince Madoc. And he came from Wales.

Among those that *did* come from Asia, there is now little cultural similarity with Asian peoples, with the exception of the Siberian peoples and the Eskimos or Inuits. Indeed, very few Native Americans have retained *all* their culture, although, as we know, many try to preserve important cultural artefacts, traditions and ceremonies. Domination of one culture by another is seen the world over, of course, and has led over the years—and still leads—to strife and bloodshed. Even in the areas where things aren't quite so dramatic, there is still a feeling of being subjugated to another culture.

I can't help drawing an analogy with the Welsh, and how many Welsh people feel about the dominance—in ancient times and modern—of England. While the Welsh language is enjoying a minor renaissance, it is still not the official language of Wales, which is, after all, still a part of the UK and has no say in its own political destiny. The American Indians became US citizens in 1924, so they, too, can no longer claim political autonomy.

As for our language, Welsh has been waning in the face of English for several centuries, though there have been notable periods when it seemed otherwise—for instance, when great numbers of ordinary people began to learn to read and write in Welsh. This was no doubt encouraged by the Welsh translation of Bible in 1588, the Calvinistic Methodist revival and the spread of the Sunday-school movement in the eighteenth century. All these factors very probably did a good deal to arrest the decline for a time. And the decline is to some extent being held in

The meeting of two cultures: Harry Sitting Bear and the author at an ancient burial chamber in north Wales.

check now, with Welsh being widely taught in schools, and many subjects taught through the medium of Welsh. There are also books and periodicals and a quango, the Welsh Language Board which, oversees the use of the Welsh language alongside English in official documents. Nevertheless, we knew a lot in Wales about struggling to keep a culture and a language alive.

When Stacey, Matthew and Craig heard their mum and dad talking about Indians, and particularly about the Mandans and their link with Wales, they, too, were fascinated and were as eager as we were to find out more.

Chapter Three

Sleepy lagoon

Mary, William's daughter, saw us first as we approached the house in Rarotonga in the Cook Islands. 'Tony, Cathy, you came.'

She hugged us all and tears welled up in her eyes. She seemed not to believe that we were really there.

'*Peea ua koe*,' said Cathy, using some local Maori she'd picked up on her last visit. Mary began to laugh and replied, '*Meitaki maata*.' Roughly translated, the exchange between the two women was, 'How are you?' 'Very good.'

Our old friend William did not look so bright. He had aged considerably. He wore dark glasses and sat in a chair. His hair was white and white bristles covered his face. He'd lost about three stone in weight. To put it mildly, he was a different man from when we'd known him on our 1993 sojourn, and when he'd done so much to help make our stay a reality.

However, he rose from his chair and greeted us enthusiastically. He told us that Tapu had been ill for some time, but was now 'out of pain, and in peace'.

We learned in conversations, sitting on William's veranda, that he'd suffered from fish poisoning. Early symptoms had been itchy skin and a stomach that swelled so much that he looked nine months pregnant. He'd been in hospital for three months.

We talked with him for a long time, mulling over the things that had happened to us a few years earlier, remembering how we'd lived on the island of Maina in as self-sufficient a way it's possible to imagine. He looked very tired and we were reluctant to put a strain on him with our endless chatter about the past, and so eventually we left him asleep on the veranda, telling Mary we'd call again tomorrow.

Rarotonga hadn't changed. We drove into town, still marvelling at this mountainous and fertile island, with its bungalow-type houses, each surrounded by lush vegetation and fruit trees—an island with a circumference of twenty miles, housing a population of around ten thousand.

We visited other old friends and on the following day returned to see William. He told us he'd had a message from his son in New Zealand, saying that the headstone wouldn't be ready until the New Year. And, while our journey hadn't exactly been wasted, we wouldn't get a chance to see it after all. This was early December.

Well, we did have some time on our hands. We had made the necessary arrangements for the postponement of our trip to North Dakota to see the Mandan Indians. I looked at Cathy. She looked at me. We each knew what the other was thinking.

Maina!

The children had spent such a lot of time here in the islands in 1993 and 1994, and the place seemed almost like home. Craig now thirteen, with his sun-bleached blond hair, was almost going native in his eagerness to settle again into island life. He insisted on feeding William's pigs and climbing for coconuts.

Matthew, now nine and with his mother's looks and a freckled face, was always seeking adventure. He was very much looking forward to visiting the Mandans, and we talked often of our impending trip. But a more immediate trip back to 'our' island now captured all his enthusiasm. We just couldn't get him to stay still. He raced around, asking 'When are we going?' and 'How long will it take?'

We booked an inter-island flight on Air Raro, to take us to Aitutaki. From there a small motorboat journey would take us to Maina. The plane was a twenty-four-seater, not the most comfortable, but it got us to Aitutaki in forty-five minutes—a lot faster than going by boat all the way. The view of the lagoon by air was breathtaking, and the colours contrasted beautifully. Everything was so well defined, as though someone had tweaked the contrast control on the TV to its absolute best.

We had made arrangements in Rarotonga with William's brother Palmers to take us out to Maina itself. And, after loading our stuff on to the boat, we were on our way once again. Back to our island.

The clear lagoon with its multi-coloured inhabitants never ceased to amaze me. This time we had taken care to cover up well. Craig and I got severely burnt the previous time: a lesson learned! And the marks are still on our bodies and faces to prove it.

'Look, Dad,' Craig called from the front of the boat, 'Maina!'

I put my hands up to shield my eyes from the blazing sun—and, sure enough, there was Maina, 'our' island, seemingly materializing before us. At first it looked small and indeterminate in the large turquoise lagoon. But, as you approach, the beauty of the island reveals itself; the lush green of the luxuriant palm fronds and many shrubs, and the brilliant, bleached sand complement the pellucid waters.

Craig in his hammock, enjoying the good life.

Soon we were on that hot white sand, watching as Palmers and the boat sailed out of sight.

'Come on,' Craig shouted eagerly. 'Let's put the tent up.' And he made his way to the place on top of a small sandy bank where our tent had been before.

'Craig,' I said (I thought it was about time I took command), 'you and Matthew clear the bits of wood and shells away. It's got to be flat before we can put the tent up, remember?'

Soon the tent was erected, and it was as though we'd never been away.

The days passed, and we got into a routine. But there was something about the boys that was different. They seemed preoccupied. Then, one night as we sat around the campfire, Matthew asked, 'Craig, do the Indians live in tents?'

32

'They're not tents,' Craig answered with that disdain that's always reserved for younger siblings. 'They're tepees.'

'Well, do they live in tepees, then?'

'I don't think so,' he said. 'They live in houses.'

'I'd rather live in a tepee than a house,' Matthew replied, his eyes lighting up at the thought of it.

There had been a lot of talk about American Indians over the previous few days. Perhaps I should have spotted sooner that the forthcoming trip to North Dakota was at the forefront of the boys' minds.

This was to be our first Christmas on the island. In some ways, I wished it could be the first of many. In others, I didn't, because I knew we had other things to explore.

Cathy and I had shown the forethought to get some simple presents for the children. These had been already wrapped and—with some difficulty—hidden from them. We made decorations from paper, the children colouring the paper and Cathy cutting out the shapes: stars, bells, candles. She then threaded cotton through the tops, and we tied them to the low-hanging fronds of a small coconut tree.

On Christmas Eve, Cathy and I stole away to where we'd hidden the presents, and put them under our decorated coconut tree. Stacey had been curious about how Santa would arrive on an island, but Cathy had reassured her that Santa was magic, and knew where all the girls and boys were at Christmas. And, if she was a good girl, he wouldn't forget to come to Maina.

And he didn't. On Christmas Day all the kids were excited—and didn't seem to mind that they had only two presents each.

There were the usual high-spirited questions: 'What've you got?' 'A rugby ball and some figure men. What've *you* got?' 'A U2 book and a game called Careers.' 'Look what I got!' (this from Stacey, ripping paper off her presents), 'An Indian doll and a bucket and spade.'

'You can make proper sand castles now, Stace,' I said to her, remembering the last time, in 1993, when all she'd had was half a coconut shell.

New Year's Eve arrived. We'd been on the island for quite some time. Palmers would be coming for us in a few days. I wanted to stay, to tell him to leave us here, to abandon plans for my research and just become a castaway again, like the Swiss Family Robinson, living off the bounty of nature without a care.

I even broached the subject with Cathy. We could just . . . well, stay, couldn't we? Forget our trip to the USA. Be self-sufficient again on our desert island.

Cathy had other ideas. She and the kids had been restless from the start. She'd even told me that, if I decided to stay, she and the kids would be leaving without me.

'But I thought this was what we wanted,' I said.

'It is,' she said, 'but not for the kids. If it was just you and me it would be OK, but it's not enough for the children.'

'OK,' I said. I know there was disappointment in my voice, but I too could feel new horizons beckoning. 'If you want to leave, we'll go.'

Seen from a desert island, the vastness of the Pacific Ocean sleeps at night—and the Universe takes its place. A mighty blackness, sequinned with stars, that seems to suck you into it. I lay in the night, contemplating our future, our paradise here and our original intention to try to shed new light on a mystery.

The following day, as I was fishing in the lagoon with Cathy, remarking on the refreshingly cool breeze that brought respite from the intense heat, we saw a small motorboat coming towards is.

'Is that Palmers?' Cathy asked.

'I think so,' I said. 'Looks like his boat.'

Ten minutes later, Palmers was standing on the beach with us.

'I've come to take you off the island,' he said.

'How did you know we'd decided to leave early?' I asked, wondering if Cathy had spoken to him before we'd left Aitutaki, and I'd been the last to know of it.

'I *didn't* know,' Palmers said. 'But there's been a cyclone warning on the radio. That's why I came.'

'Oh, great,' I said. 'That's *all* we need.'

And within the hour we were loading the last of our things on to the boat.

'I'll miss the island,' I told Cathy as it became a speck in the distance.

'I know,' she said. 'But we can come back when the children are older—just the two of us.' She gave my hand a squeeze, and smiled. Perhaps the gods hadn't meant us to stay. Not yet.

'Yes,' I said, probably to myself—I don't remember. 'Yes, we will. We'll come back.'

Chapter Four

The day we went to Bangor

When we got home, Cathy and I decided to visit the site of the burial place of Prince Madoc's father, Owain Gwynedd, at Bangor. While Owain was fighting battles for his people and their land, Madoc was displaying a love for the sea, his views on many things differing greatly from those of his father. It's thought that it was his ever-growing disillusionment with matters at home and the quarrelling among his brothers that eventually drove him from Wales.

The name Owain Gwynedd may be found in various history books as Owain (or Owen) ap Gruffydd or ap Gryffydd. Both are pronounced the same, with the 'dd' pronounced as a voiced 'th', as it is in 'the', and the 'u' as the 'i' in 'bid'. For our purposes here we'll call him Owain Gwynedd. He was the last king of north Wales to be known as such and helped to advance Welsh independence against the dominance of the Normans and the English.

He had a brother called Cadwaladr, and together they led three expeditions during 1136–37 against the English stronghold at Ceredigion to the south. They managed to ravage this region, and established Welsh castles themselves there.

When Owain's father died in 1137, Owain ascended the throne of north Wales. During the reign of King Stephen, which ended in 1154, Owain ruled successfully, extending his boundaries almost to the city of Chester.

It was Henry II, who succeeded Stephen, who challenged Owain in 1157—but failed in the ensuing battle. Eventually an agreement was reached: Owain would withdraw to Rhuddlan and the River Clwyd, and render homage. These terms were kept until 1165, when Owain combined forces with Rhys ap Gruffydd, his nephew and then the Prince of South Wales, and with another Owain, Owain Cyfeiliog (c.1130–97), of Powys and moved against Henry's forces in Wales.

Henry and his forces were defeated by a combination of strong Welsh forces and bad weather at the Battle of Berwyn. As a result of such victories, the Welsh regained control of the border country. Thus Owain regained castles at Basingwerk and Rhuddlan, which had been previously taken by Henry, and re-established the borders of Gwynedd on the Dee estuary.

The independence he secured in north Wales was maintained during Owain's lifetime, but succeeding generations, of course, would not be up to the task of retaining independence for Wales. In particular, one son—Dafydd, Madoc's brother—brought about a regime that disillusioned and terrorised many. He outlawed and exiled some of his brothers and may well have threatened Madoc's life.

Briefly, I've gone some way to setting the scene for the period during which Prince Madoc decided Wales was not the place for him. So it was that Madoc left the land where his father Owain had been a great Welsh legend, and became a leader of his people not in Wales but across the Atlantic. Ironically, Madoc's descendants, and those of the people he took with him to America, had several hundred years of independence, while Wales lost hers in

1282 with the death of Llewelyn, '*ein Llyw olaf*'—our last leader.

At the cathedral in Bangor, where Owain Gwynedd was buried, we saw a shrine to the great leader, but not the original tomb, for Owain's remains were removed from the cathedral not long after the burial—because of great controversy over an illegal marriage he had made to his cousin. Although his bones had to be removed from the building itself, the Bishop ensured that they were still secretly buried in consecrated ground, just outside the building. So exactly where the remains now lie, we could not be sure, but in that grand and ancient cathedral it was not difficult to imagine the presence of the mighty leader. I remembered reading a description of him that was written at the time of his death (in *Brut y Tywysogion, The Chronicle of the Princes*) which praised him as a 'man who was of great goodness and very great nobility and wisdom, the bulwark of all Wales, after innumerable victories, and unconquered from his youth, without ever having refused anyone that for which he asked.'

Cathy and I left the burial site in Bangor, and began the long train journey home. As I looked out of the carriage on to the sprawling countryside shooting past us, I reflected more on those tumultuous times, and how different Madoc's life must have been after he had made his decision to go away for good.

He was a man with a love of the sea; he was an adventurer; he had been to America not once but twice.

On his first expedition he had left from Abercerrig, near Abergele on the north Wales coast—spelt in several old documents as Aber-Kerrick Gwynyon. My research

The cathedral at Bangor, burial place of Owain Gwynedd.

tells me he visited the Bahamas either while travelling to or from America.

When he arrived back in Britain, he set out to borrow—or perhaps steal—his much-needed ships to carry his three hundred followers on what would be his last journey from Wales. Most sources cite ten ships, but it's interesting that a popular and still much-quoted poem from the last century gives it at thirteen. The poet Ceiriog (1832-1887) describes Madoc's departure thus:

Wele'n cychwyn dair ar ddeg
O longau bach ar fore teg:
Wele Madog ddewr ei fron
Yn gapten ar y llynges hon.

Translated, the verse runs: See yonder thirteen little ships, setting out one fine morning; and see Madoc, brave of heart, the captain of his fleet.

However many ships he had in his fleet, it appears that this time he set off from Lundy Island in the Bristol Channel, a granite island, now the site of an important seabird colony. Eventually, Madoc arrived in Mobile Bay, Alabama.

But there is some confusion over whether he actually did steal ships or join forces with the Danes. As we'll see later, he was very friendly with the Danes, he had Viking blood in his veins, and there's a school of thought that says he would have travelled on one of their ships. Another story has it that the ship he left Wales on was the *Gwenan Gorn*, said to have been one of the ships King Henry discovered missing.

I suppose we'll never know—nor should we care. It is a minute detail compared with the enormity of what I believe happened subsequently—the founding of a community of people in the New World whose blood line would reach to the present day, and a community of American Indians in North Dakota.

Chapter Five

Big country

We were almost there—just one more connecting flight and we would be in North Dakota. Minot to be exact—where all our plans had meant us to be. But there was still that one more connecting flight, and we were still in Minneapolis in southeast Minnesota.

We stood in a long queue with many other visitors on their way to many other parts of America, all of us waiting to get through immigration, eyeing each other but trying not to be seen doing it—the way you do in doctors' waiting rooms, or when you're standing doing nothing except shuffling slowly forward in an airport queue. All you can do is be patient—which was fine for Cathy and me, but when you have three children in tow, all keen for adventure, patience can be in short supply.

As we stood, a dog was led around by officials, sniffing everyone's hand luggage.

'Next!' Eventually it was our turn. We moved to the desk and stood in front of the immigration officer, feeling as if we were being scrutinized. She seemed friendly enough. She even smiled at the children. But something in her eyes told me she would be asking questions.

Cathy handed over our tickets and passports.

'Your ticket says you're going to Minot,' she said, eyeing us one by one. 'Why are you going there?' She glanced again at the children. 'There's nothing much up there for a family,' she said.

I told her we'd been invited to visit a reservation, and her smiling face changed.

'Why?' she asked. 'For what reason?'

'I'm—I mean *we*, Cathy, my wife, and I—we're carrying out research,' I stammered. 'I'm looking into the Madoc legend. You know, the theory about the connection between the Welsh and the Mandans.' I didn't need to explain that we were Welsh. She'd clocked my Swansea accent by now. Even if she couldn't pinpoint it to Wales's second city, I guessed she'd had no difficulty in telling we were from Wales. I suppose I expected a friendlier greeting, and, while I can't say she was positively aggressive, I didn't expect the sarcasm that followed.

'I suppose an Indian told you this.' It wasn't really a question. I didn't know whether she expected an answer or her remarks were purely rhetorical. I decided on the patient approach.

'No,' I said, slowly and deliberately, trying not to show that I was beginning to feel annoyed by her attitude. 'It's a well-known legend, and I hope to prove it.' But this seemed to disturb her even more and she began to bombard us with what seemed irrelevant questions.

'How much money do you have?' she asked. Then, 'Do your children have permission to be away from school?' Cathy and I parried her questions as well as we could. Finally she flabbergasted us with the assertion: 'I know my history. You English hung Guy Fawkes, didn't you?'

After our exasperation had died down a little, we allowed ourselves to be amused by the immigration officer's manner. 'Oh, well,' I said, 'if that's what turns her on . . .' We English, indeed! We turned our attention once again to what had become a mission—made more determined now by the attitude of the immigration officer, who seemed to be ridiculing what we were setting out to prove.

Another example, I thought, of people refusing to open their minds to possibilities. After all, a lot of established historical credos have been debunked over the years. Was it so difficult to be open to the shedding of some new light on an old story? If it only got people talking and going back to their researches, it would achieve something.

At least it gave us all something to talk about during our connecting flight—which, because of the hassle, we almost missed.

But soon we stepped off our Northwest Airlines plane and on to this vast North Dakota land.

Stacey and Matthew were excited and seemed to think we'd be continuing our journey on horseback, through great expanses of wilderness.

'You've been watching too much television,' I said. 'We'll be going the modern way: by car.'

'Boor-ing!' Matthew intoned.

We soon discovered just how many hundreds of miles separated the various places we needed to visit, so we had no option but to hire a car. Mind you, the idea of a horseback journey did have a certain appeal. I guessed that it was one of those ideas that wouldn't really go away until we'd had a spell in the saddle. But for now, it had to be a blue Ford. Off we went.

We drove for what seemed like endless miles down a long stretch of road called Broadway, on Expressway 83, and then turned off on to Route 23, suddenly entering a new world. More than 400,000 acres of Indian territory. It was as if the old Wild West had come alive—not for its wildness, perhaps, but certainly for the breathtaking vastness of this seemingly illimitable expanse of prairie.

In spite of our previous travels, something about this sweeping tract filled us all with a sense of awe, reverence almost, for something so unspoiled and beautiful.

I was not long in these thoughts before I was brought down to earth by Craig's voice. 'Dad, we've been travelling for over an hour and we haven't seen anybody.'

'We've just passed a raccoon,' said Matthew drily.

I turned to Cathy and smiled. 'This is great, isn't it?' I said.

'Yes,' she said. 'I never expected it to be so unspoiled.'

We drove on a little further. I was keen to see a trail that is a part of our jigsaw—this was where the legendary travellers Lewis and Clark had once travelled.

Meriwether Lewis (1774–1809) and William Clark (1770–1838) jointly led an expedition to explore the Louisiana Territory that President Thomas Jefferson had purchased from Napoleon of France (it was named Louisiana after Louis XIV). Jefferson had also acquired most of the great plains area—with the exception of Texas—from the Mississippi River west to the Rocky Mountains. Lewis was Jefferson's secretary and had been a captain in the army. Clark was the brother of George Rogers Clark, who'd been a hero in the American Revolution.

Lewis and Clark were commissioned to explore the newly acquired area—from the Mississippi River to the Pacific coast, most of which was known only to the natives—and report on its nature and value. The expedition set out from St Louis in 1804, crossing North America and reaching the mouth of the Columbia river on the Pacific coast in 1805. It returned to St Louis in 1806.

The group was made up of interpreters, soldiers and frontiersmen, among others, and even Lewis's Newfoundland dog, Seaman, accompanied them.

During their travelling, Lewis and Clark and their fellow discoverers came across different cultures in what was, to them, a new land. While others had been there before, it was the Lewis and Clark expedition that first mapped the land. They carried out their explorations until the end of autumn, when they stopped for the winter, and built huts of logs on the land of the Mandan and Hidatsa tribes. They spent the winter months studying the friendly Indians and learning from them.

Something struck Lewis and Clark as strange about the Mandans. They seemed to be lighter of skin than the other tribes they encountered, and their tongue and dialect seemed altogether different.

Their expedition would not have been as successful, however, without the help of a teenage Shoshone Indian girl called Sakakawea (Bird Woman). Sakakawea was captured at the age of twelve by the Hidatsa people, who sold her to a Frenchman named Charbonneau, who subsequently took her as his wife.

Charbonneau was engaged as an interpreter by Lewis and Clark for their journey through Indian country, and he insisted that Sakakawea accompany them, even though, by this time, they had a baby son, Baptiste.

Sakakawea helped to guide them safely through her

native Shoshone land, and was largely responsible for much of the material assistance the expedition received from her people. She also pointed out to them the Bozeman Pass and other points that proved to be valuable to the expedition.

In 1801, Charbonneau and Sakakawea took Baptiste to St Louis, because Clark had expressed an interest in caring for the boy's education.

Subsequently, Sakakawea and Charbonneau returned from the West Coast to the Knife River villages, and it's believed they went to St Louis in 1810 to take Baptiste to Captain Clark so he could care for the boy's education. In 1811, a boat was sent upriver by Manuel Lisa, who wanted to establish a fur-trading post among the Arikara, and an author called Henry Brackenridge recalled that a white man and an Indian woman were aboard:

> We have on board a Frenchman named Charbonneau, with his wife, an Indian woman of the Snake nation, both of whom accompanied Lewis and Clark to the Pacific and were of great service. The woman, a good creature, of a mild and gentle disposition was greatly attached to the whites, whose manners and airs she tries to imitate; but she had become sickly and longed to revisit her native country; her husband also, who had spent many years amongst the Indians, was becoming weary of civilized life.

There's some contention about the time of Sakakawea's death. Some say she died young, in 1812, of a putrifying fever, and some authorities believe she died an old woman in 1884 at Fort Washakie, Wyoming.

The author at the Statue of Sakakawea, Bismarck.

In memory of this brave young Shoshone girl, there is a bronze statue of her and her baby son on the State Capitol grounds at Bismarck, the capital of North Dakota, which sits just across the Missouri from the city of Mandan, some miles down river from Lake Sakakawea.

And it is the Mandan connection that interested me when I read about Lewis and Clark. Their observations on the Mandan race are among many that point to a link between the Mandans and Madoc more than eight hundred years ago.

As a footnote to the Lewis and Clark expedition, I might add that in 1807 Lewis was made Governor of Louisiana Territory, and Clark became Governor of Missouri Territory in 1813. Later, after Missouri had become a state, Clark was appointed Superintendent of Indian Affairs, and was popular among the natives, because, it is said, he always tried to treat them fairly.

Chapter Six

Indian country

The town of Minot (pronounced *my*-nott), into which we flew, is about 160 miles from the city of Mandan and home to more than 34,000 people. The houses we saw in Minot were all detached, most of a cabin-style design, and the first thing we noticed about the people was that they were very friendly, many of them greeting us spontaneously with a sociable 'Hi'. Compared with that of most American cities and towns, traffic here is slight. This was just as well: it was the first time I'd driven on the 'wrong' side of the road. We were bound for New Town, which is in the Fort Berthold reservation.

The reservation is not the original Fort Berthold. On 24 December 1862 the Sioux burnt down Fort Berthold. Fort Atkinson was owned by the American Fur Company, who had owned the Fort Berthold fur-trading post, so Fort Atkinson was now occupied and renamed Fort Berthold.

At New Town we were looking for the Tribal Administration Office, and had come to see one Ed Lone Fight. I had contacted him by letter before our visit and he had invited us to come to the reservation, saying he would be glad to meet us any time. We saw the signpost for the reservation office. It was a one-storey building. Immediately we were met by the friendly but curious looks of the Native Americans who were around the main entrance. A man who seemed to be in charge of the reception area approached us.

'Can I help you?'

'Yes,' I said. 'We're looking for Ed Lone Fight.' I produced a copy of the letter I'd received from him. 'Is he here?'

'His office is down here,' said the official. 'Follow me.' And we did. The five of us trailed after him, feeling a little self-conscious under the stares of the Native Americans around us. We went down a small corridor until we came to two native women standing at a doorway. Our guide pointed to the older of them and said, 'That lady will help you.'

I smiled and thanked him; he nodded and walked away.

I approached the woman he'd pointed out to us and showed her the letter.

'Ed's not here today,' she said. I think she could see the disappointment on my face. 'He's in a meeting in Washington. He won't be able to meet with you until tomorrow, but I'm his assistant, Sue. Maybe I can help you'.

I told her we were here to do research on the connection between the Mandans and the Welsh. She listened with interest, then said, 'OK, I'll try to put you in touch with some people who may be able to help you.' But first, she asked, would we like to watch the Appreciation Day celebration? It would add some colour and interest to our researches, she assured us.

Well, yes, why not? I said as much, then looked at Cathy. She shrugged, smiled and gave me a 'Why not?' sort of look. Sue seemed happy with our decision, and showed us into a small hall, with chairs set out in rows facing two long tables at the front.

We learned that this was a special occasion in honour

of Dr Wilson, who had arrived from Canada forty-three years before and had been the doctor to the natives here ever since. We watched, fascinated, as first there was a naming ceremony, in which Dr Wilson and his wife, Lilian, were given Indian names in honour of their service to the community. Dr Wilson was named One Who Heals, while Lilian was given the title Woman Who Assists Many.

Dr Wilson, One Who Heals.

Then there were tributes from tribal leaders and Dr Wilson was praised for all his achievements over the years. Plaques were presented to him and his wife, along with pictures, a quilt and a spectacular and resplendent headdress.

But the climax—for me, at any rate—was the tribal dancing that followed. Three Native Americans played drums with such energy and emotion, and yet with the sort of disciplined precision that has you feeling the warmth of nascent tears behind your eyes. They also sang in their native tongue, luring us, transporting us, into a completely different world. I looked around at Cathy, and I could see that she was moved, too. Even the children kept their eyes firmly on the players and dancers, mesmerized, captivated by the driving rhythms that pummelled the air and the dervishlike whirling and spinning of the dancers. It was an experience I'll not forget in a hurry.

After the excitement was over, we were given an old medicine bottle containing sweets, as a memento of the day. Sue asked us to wait while she went off to see someone else, and we sat in a sort of stunned silence, with those drumbeats still ringing in our ears, and observed the people around us.

They reminded me very much of the Cook Islanders, with their warm smiles and trusting ways. As I looked at my children and my wife, I thought how, just four months before, we were all in the Cook Islands, dressed in shorts and T-shirts. Craig, then thirteen, and Matthew, who was nine, were husking coconuts while Cathy and I fished. I thought of how we'd all sat in the clear lagoon trying to cool off after our crab races, under the blistering sun.

Now we were sitting in our thick coats, hats and gloves in temperatures of five degrees. A far cry from the Pacific, but as far as I was concerned it was just as fulfilling.

My reverie was interrupted by Cathy. She always seems to do that—nudge me into wakefulness when my mind has drifted off to another universe.

'Where d'you think Sue's got to?' she asked.

'Dunno,' I replied. 'Probably seeing some people about us.'

No sooner were the words out of my mouth than she appeared.

'Come with me,' she said enthusiastically, like a child wanting to show Mum and Dad a new toy. 'I have someone I'd like you to meet.'

We followed her to a table at the side of the hall, and there sat a distinguished grey-haired Native American. Sue introduced us.

'Tony, Cathy, this is Luther Edward Grinnell,' she said. 'He's half Mandan, half Hidatsa.'

It seemed odd to be introduced to someone and be told his tribal lineage in the same breath. Not the sort of introduction we were used to in Swansea.

'Hello,' Cathy and I said in unison.

'Hi.' Luther beamed at us as he stood up to shake our hands. He was a tall man—over six foot—and obviously strong and powerful. His short hair was silver grey and it topped a friendly, welcoming, bespectacled pair of eyes canopied by dark, bushy brows. 'Come outside,' he said.

We followed Luther outside the hall, pulling our collars up against the cold. He led us towards the bank of the river, the Missouri. 'Your children are happy children,' he said as we walked. Although the day was cold, it was sunny and clear, crisp and invigorating. 'Let's sit here,' he said at last.

I expected that the children would want to wander off and explore, but they seemed fascinated by our newfound friend. Stacey drank water from the round flask we had brought with us. She offered some to Luther.

'Ah, water, yes,' he said, displaying a sort of reverence for a commodity we very much take for granted. He drank, and handed the flask back to Stacey, who looked down shyly as he smiled his thanks to her.

'Sue tells me you are Celtics,' Luther said at last. He had seemed in no hurry to get down to the business of our trip. It was as though he was saying by this gesture that we need not be hurried, that there was all the time in the world, and we could afford to be relaxed and tell our story in our own good time.

We told him why we were here, that we had been sent a letter by Ed Lone Fight, whom we were due to meet the following day, that we were chasing a legend that some historians had tried to debunk. Luther nodded, as if he were expecting all this, knowing with our every word what we were going to say next.

Then Luther began to tell us his own story.

Chapter Seven

Luther's story

'My grandfather,' Luther Grinnell began solemnly, but with the practised voice of the storyteller, 'had a warrior name: Blackfox. As an elder his name was Blackchest. He told me of the moving islands, the ships that came over here and landed in our country, and he said the people who would become the Mandans landed at the mouth of the Mississippi river.'

By now our family group was captivated, and Luther had spoken only a few sentences.

'My grandfather said they went up the Ohio River Valley—clear to the end of it. The land wasn't any good for planting corn, so they came back, and when they settled in North Dakota other Indians noticed that some Mandans had blue eyes, and some had blond hair.'

Luther explained that, hundreds of years later—in 1738—an explorer and fur trader called Pierre Gaultier de la Verendrye came looking for these people, having become intrigued by stories he'd heard. He visited the village of what he called 'the Mantannes'.

'He came right up here, and at a river called Little Knife River he found the Hidatsa tribe, and thought they were the Mandans. But there was a misunderstanding due to the sign language, and they found that the Mandans were down river. Verendrye went down river and found the Mandans. He stayed with them and wrote about the differences between them and other Native American peoples.'

What was significant, Luther said, was that he found the language of this strange tribe to be very similar to that of the Welsh people. And there was a striking similarity in the way they built their homes.

'When the Mandans eventually settled down here in Bismarck and Mandan,' said Luther, 'they had earth lodges. That looks like a Celtic-type thing of old, you know.'

Luther then went on to speak about the city of Mandan.

'It's right across the river from Bismarck, about a hundred sixty-five miles from here. Bismarck is our capital city here in North Dakota, and Mandan is where the Mandans used to live. There are no Indians there now, but they do have some earth lodges. There's a place called Fort Lincoln. The lodges are just left of there. Fort Lincoln is where Custer—General Custer—where his fort was. He didn't get killed there: he got killed in Montana—Little Big Horn.'

Luther paused a moment, and looked at the sky. We were so fascinated by now with his story that we had almost forgotten how cold it was.

'The Mandans lived in earth lodges,' he repeated, 'and I'm guessing about 1890, because the last village—which was called Like-a-fish-hook Village, near Garrison—is under water now. That place had earth lodges, too. They were moved to Elbowoods—which is also now inundated—around 1890, and they lived in cabins after that. There were only about four earth lodges left on the reservation at that time. They built new ones as they moved up here. That was probably in the 1890s or 1900s, when they had those, 'cause I was born in 1922 and those old Indians were still living then, in 1922.

'We're Americans now, but a lot of people don't feel good about it. They were independent until they were conquered. They've never really settled to it spiritually, you know, so they still have some of their culture, still have some of their tradition, and they still have their language.

'I can speak Hidatsa fluently,' Luther continued. 'But I didn't learn to speak English till I was seven years old.'

I took advantage of a pause in Luther's monologue and asked, 'What's happened to the Mandan language now? Have they lost it?'

'There are a few left who can still speak Mandan,' Luther said.

'On this reservation?' I asked, hoping against hope that the answer would be yes. And it was.

'Yes, in Mandan country at Twin Buttes. See, this reservation is divided into five segments, because the lake, Sakakawea, comes right through the middle of it, and cuts it off into five districts. The southern district—about a hundred miles from here—that's the Twin Buttes area.'★

Luther said there were several Indians there who still knew the Mandan language. Suddenly an image sprang into my mind of a group of people determined to cut themselves off from modernity and live according to their proud traditions. I couldn't resist asking Luther, 'Are there any reservations in America that still live as they used to? Do any of them live as they did in the past? And have any kept their old traditions?'

★ *Butte* is chiefly a North American term. The word is French for mound, and that's just what it is: a high-sided hill, and in this case taken to mean one that's isolated.

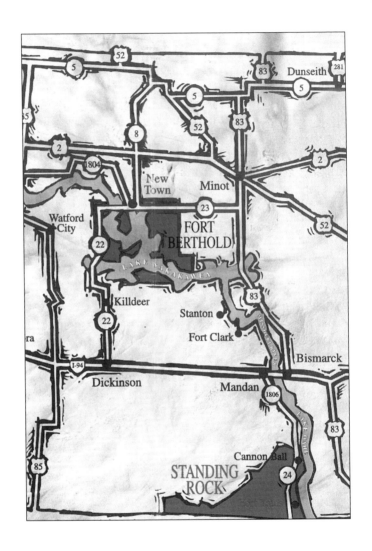

'No, no,' said Luther, not surprised at my question. He'd probably been asked it a hundred times before. 'They're into modern technology. They farm with machinery, harvest with machinery. But some of them still carry on their gardens like they used to, way back. I do that. I put in a garden. I've got some squash right now that's Hidatsa, and I've got some Hidatsa beans and some Mandan corn.'

'What about buffalo?' I asked. 'Are there still any buffalo?'

'Buffalo?' Luther smiled. 'Oh, yeah, we have a buffalo herd. It belongs to the tribe. We have a big fence around it, along the lake south of here—about thirty, thirty-five miles away.'

'I thought a lot of them were destroyed,' I said. I seemed to remember reading that they were virtually extinct in the wild state in the USA, although some were preserved in parks such as Yellowstone, and herds of them roam Theodore Roosevelt National Park in North Dakota. The North American buffalo is actually a bison, of course, and is of a different genus—but tends to be called buffalo by many people, nevertheless. Luther read my thoughts.

'Yes,' he said, 'they *were* practically extinct, but they began programmes to start rebreeding them. Now they're scattered all over quite a bit.'

'What's your Indian name?' I asked him.

'My Indian name is Naganahosh,' he said, barely concealing a mischievous smile that seemed to say, Go on, get your tongue around *that* one.

'You're going to have to spell that one,' Cathy said, laughing. She was taking notes. Luther spelled it out.

'It's a medicine name,' he said. He explained that much 'medicine' in American Indian terms has to do with a sacred bundle, which is made up of secret clan items and other things, such as turtle shell. That bundle has a caretaker within the family and is passed from father to son, and through sacred ritual, prayers and songs, its custodian receives gifts and a special name.

'That's how I got my name,' said Luther. 'It alludes to a horse. This bundle had to do with horses and sacred medicine.'

During the rituals, Luther was blessed, in a ceremony meant to bestow on him good luck and protection throughout his life, a good mind and the ability to help his people in whatever problems they have.

'And I'm doing all of that. It just comes natural. I never even looked for it. It just drops in my lap every time I turn around.'

It struck me that here were we, Cathy, me and the kids—a family in search of a legend—trying to make a link between this man and a Welsh prince, and here was Luther talking about something that seemed so alien. But such are the twists and turns of fortune, and it was an awesome thought that, during those dark days of Welsh troubles more than eight hundred years ago, one man's decision to make a journey would lead to a fork in history. One people would emerge thousands of miles away, carrying with them some of the distinguishing characteristics of physiognomy and language of the Welsh. Mandan culture—impacted by influences of Sioux and other native peoples, and ultimately White America— would develop along its own course, while at home in

Wales, Welsh culture too would be susceptible to influences from outside itself.

While the Mandans are said to be of Sioux stock, we'll see that that influence was a part of the life journey of a people who began life before they met up with the Sioux and eventually split from them, a people who now like to remember their links with a land far away in both distance and culture from the one they call home.

Luther could see, I think, that my mind was racing, taking in what he had told us about linguistic links and French explorers, about earth lodges and sacred bundles. He seemed to know what my next question would be.

'Have you heard of the Prince Madoc theory?' I asked. 'That he left Wales and came here?'

'Yes, I believe that,' he said, 'because those Celts, they were in ocean-going vessels. They went all the way around into the Mediterranean area and down the coast of Africa and around England, Scotland and Wales—all around—and they had big tremendous ships.' So it was entirely possible, he seemed to be saying, that they came here, to North America.

'There's a plaque at Mobile Bay in Alabama,' I said, 'saying that Madoc landed there in 1170. Do you know of it?'

'Well, you see, Alabama has a little spur,' said Luther, and he took our map and traced along it with his finger. 'This is Florida, and this is Alabama. Mobile, Alabama, is here. So, anywhere along in that coast, all past the Mississippi, there's a lot of bays and bayous. You know, you could land almost anyplace through there. And according to Verendrye, the French explorer, the Mandans started their journey from around this area.'

We told Luther that we had been reading about Verendrye, and that the village of 'the Mantannes' he mentioned was at first thought to have been a camp on the Missouri near the present site of New Town, which is about a hundred and fifteen miles northwest of Mandan. However, latterday historians have determined that he reached the Missouri near Bismarck and Mandan. Luther nodded. We knew that telling him about local history was like the proverbial teaching of Granny to suck eggs. But he knew I was clarifying my own thoughts—making sure I was getting it right.

'Yes,' he said, and agreed that Verendrye was one of many who had said that the Mandan and Welsh languages were similar.

Then he gave us the names of three people in the Twin Buttes area who might be of further help. 'Talk to Edwin Benson, Lida Chase or Ernest Stone,' he said. 'They'll set you straight.' And we *would* be speaking to Edwin Benson, but that would not be until a second visit to this fascinating part of the world—a visit we were not at this moment aware would come about.

We reminded Luther of our letter from Ed Lone Fight, and asked about him.

'He's part Mandan—he's got more Mandan in him than Hidatsa. See, he's my cousin. His dad's my first cousin. His dad is *Ted* Lone Fight.'

'Do any of them speak the Mandan language?' Cathy asked.

'I don't think Ed does, but those guys I told you about speak Mandan fluently.'

'Have you got horses?' Matthew suddenly blurted.

Luther smiled. The usual courtesies of conversation

were not for a kid of ten. Matthew wanted to ride, and Matthew was determined to mention horses at every available opportunity.

'Yeah,' said Luther. 'I got horses.'

'He said he'd like to ride a horse while we're here,' I offered, half apologetically.

'Well, mine are broncs. Know what that means?' Matthew looked puzzled. 'Well they're wild, and they'll buck you off. I don't have any gentle ones, but I'm working on one. It's too bad I didn't have 'im tame already. You could ride 'im, sure. But he's not tame yet.'

'Who taught you how to ride?' Cathy asked.

'My grandpa,' said Luther. 'He was a storyteller, and had hundreds of stories. I grew up listening to them, when I was a little fella like this guy here.' And with that he ruffled Matthew's hair. 'I didn't know what he was doing to me until I was in World War Two. He was teaching me to be a warrior all those years.

'The basic requisites don't sound like warriorhood at all. It has to do with honesty, courage, being trustworthy, having dignity, honour and respect, and knowing what's truthful and beautiful and fair, and what is happiness and love and so on. And when you have that ingrained into you, then you do not fear death, and that's the warrior's first requisite: not to fear death. Once they spiritually accept that, that there is a life hereafter, in the spiritual world, and it's a better world than we live in now . . .'

And Luther proceeded to tell us something about the values instilled into the young in his granddad's day, how youngsters moved through a grade system—just as they do in modern American high schools. But this was different.

'Little boys of Matthew's age had their own group. They had their own costumes, their own paint, their own songs, their own dances and rituals, and the basic thing was honesty and courage. Then, when they got bigger, they went into another study, and they had different costumes and songs and prayers. And after a number of years they went into another stage, but basically it taught the same things: honesty, courage and reverence— reverence for the divine nature of things, courage for the fact that there is another life after death, and honesty to face yourself as you really are, and to have self-control so you won't get guilt and fear. Feeling fear and hate—those things are mental blocks. If you do something wrong and you pick these things up in your mind, you become weaker. You're not as good as a warrior then.'

How did Luther feel, I wondered, about being part of a minority now? 'Your people fought very hard for the land,' I said, 'but in the end so many others came here that you just seemed to be outnumbered.'

Luther's face took on an almost melancholy mien as he spoke, slowly, deliberately.

'Yes, disease and genocide, you know. And of course warfare. See, there were thirty thousand of us: there were fifteen thousand Hidatsa and fifteen thousand Mandan. But by the early nineteen hundreds there were only eight hundred Hidatsa and two hundred Mandan left. Both together made fewer than a thousand.'

'Because of the fighting?' I asked.

'Some of it.' I thought Luther was about to say something else, so I waited a while before asking my next question.

'What do you mean by genocide?' I asked.

'Genocide. Ah, the government put out infected blankets,' he said, 'infected with smallpox—out into the tribe. And they got these blankets and they started an epidemic—and they died off from smallpox, 'cause Indians had no resistance to it. Other kinds of diseases, too. You know, like diphtheria—diphtheria was a killer — and typhoid and chickenpox.'

Then, said Luther, there were the battles.

'The Hidatsa were with General Gibbin,' he said. 'My grandpa was a scout for General Gibbin, and the Arikara were scouts for General Custer. Now everyone's heard of General George Custer, of course. He led his men into battle at Little Bighorn in Montana.'

'Custer's last stand . . .'

'Yeah, that's right. Well, the Mandans, they were with the Hidatsa. They lived together after they moved out of what they now call the Knife River Villages . . .' And Luther proceeded to tell me more about the Mandan people, and the other two tribes with whom they share their reservation.

Chapter Eight

Three's company

It was in 1846 that the Mandans and a tribe called the Gros Ventre moved up the Missouri to their present reservation area. They settled around the trading post of the American Fur Company, which was named after its founder, Bartholomew Berthold. The trading post was at a bend in the Missouri that resembled a fish-hook. True to the convention of giving things names that stemmed from a quality, the natives called it Like-a-fish-hook Bend, and the village that eventually grew up there was called Like-a-fish-hook Village.

It's a vexed question as to which of the three tribes lived there first, but it would be either the Gros Ventre or the Mandans. And the consensus seems to support the theory that it was the Mandans.

These three tribes differed from other Native Americans in that they were more settled, built permanent homes and practised agriculture instead of just hunting and gathering. I couldn't help thinking that, if the Mandans *were* the first there, it would have been their influence that led to the three tribes' agrarian way of life.

Both the Mandans and the Gros Ventre are of Sioux stock. The Mandans came here from the Ohio Valley to the east, as Luther had indicated when he was talking about the stories his grandfather had told him. This was in the fifteenth century, and they were probably already settled along the Missouri when Columbus arrived in the Americas.

The Gros Ventre originated in the Devils Lake area in North Dakota and may also have been located north among the Assiniboines in Canada. They were driven west by the marauding Sioux, reached the Missouri opposite the mouth of the Heart River and opposite the villages of the Mandans. It's known from the journals of travellers that they moved to the mouth of the Knife River before 1796.

Although 'Gros Venture' became their official name, it is a misnomer. The true name is 'Hidatsa'. They acquired the sobriquet 'Gros Ventre' because of some sort of linguistic confusion among early French fur traders. 'Gros Ventre' means 'big belly', and must have seemed an appropriate name for the Hidatsa, who, it was noticed, were rather well built.

The third tribe are the Arikara, who are of Caddoan stock and were once part of the Northern branch of the Skidi Pawnee. 'Arikara' is a Skidi word for 'horns', and these people were so named because of their practice of wearing bones in their hair. They were another tribe driven away by the Sioux.

The Assiniboines referred to the Hidatsa and Mandans as 'Sioux who go underground', an allusion to the earth lodges that are so characteristic of these tribes' history. It must have looked as if these people were disappearing into the side of a small hill.

Traditionally, earth lodges were built mainly by the women. Huge posts of cottonwood were cut during the summer before the lodge was to be built. The men would drag them to the village in the winter, over the snow and ice.

Men helped raising the heavy posts, although the

women were responsible for the whole structure. The posts were so large that twenty men were needed to raise each one.

There were four sacred foundation posts, and only certain women of the village had the right to supervise their erection. For their services, they received a soft-tanned buffalo skin and a large wooden bowl of meat.

Once the framework was in place, a thatch of willows and dried prairie grass was put over the rafters, and the entire structure was covered with loose earth or sods with the roots uppermost. There were no nails or pegs in the construction.

It would take about a week to complete the lodge, and they could be anything from thirty to sixty feet in diameter. They were durable, too, lasting anything from seven to ten years.

In the summer of 1806, one Alexander Henry stayed at the Black Cats village—one of the Mandan settlements. There's an excellent description of the earth lodge in his journals:

> A [Mandan] circular hut is spacious. I measured the one I lodged in and found it 90 feet from the door to the opposite side. The whole space is first dug out about one and one-half feet below the surface of the earth. In the center is the square fireplace, about five feet on each side, dug out about two feet below the surface of the ground flat.
>
> The lower part of the hut is constructed by erecting strong posts about six feet out of the ground, at equal distances from each other, according to the proposed size of the hut, as they are

not all the same dimensions. Upon these are laid logs as large as the posts, reaching from post to post to form the circle.

On the outer side are placed pieces of split wood seven feet long, in a slanting direction, one end resting on the ground, the other leaning against the cross-logs or beams. Upon the beams rest rafters about the thickness of a man's leg, and 12 to 15 feet long, slanting enough to drain off the rain, and laid so close to each other as to touch.

The upper ends of the rafters are supported upon stout pieces of squared timber which are supported by four thick posts about five feet in circumference, 15 feet out of the ground and 15 feet asunder, forming a square. Over these squared timbers others of equal size are laid, crossing them at right angles, leaving an opening about four feet square. This serves as chimney and window, as there are no more openings to admit light, and when it rains even this opening is covered over with a canoe bull boat to prevent the rain from injuring their gammine and earthen pots.

The whole roof is well thatched with the small willows in which the Missouri abounds, laid on to the thickness of six inches or more, fastened together in a very compact manner and well secured to the rafters. Over the whole is spread about one foot of earth, and around the wall, to the height of three or four feet, is commonly laid up earth to the thickness of three feet, for security in case of an attack and to keep out the cold.

The door is five feet broad and six feet high, with

a covered way as the door, seven feet broad and ten in length. The doors are made of raw buffalo hide stretched upon a frame and suspended by cords from one of the beams which form the circle. Every night the door is barricaded with a long piece of timber supported by two stout posts set in the ground in the inside of the hut, one on each side of the door.

Typically, around the outermost part of the inside of the lodge, would be beds, inside small tentlike affairs for privacy. There would also be a place for preparing meals, somewhere to keep the bull boats—small, tub-shaped canoes—and yet somewhere else for firewood. There would be a small corral for horses, a place for dogs and a place for animal feedstuff.

The earth lodge, then, was a sophisticated affair, probably quite cosy and self-contained. A far cry from our

An earth-lodge at Fort Berthold reservation.

modern semis with their central heating, microwave oven and the ubiquitous telly.

Among early whites who made contact with the three tribes was a Spaniard, Jacques D'Eglise, who had been licensed by the Spanish Lieutenant Governor of Illinois to hunt on the Upper Missouri. He reported that he had come across villages of Indians who went by the name of Mandan.

Probably the first fur-trading post was established in the area in 1794. This was an English company with bases in Canada: the North West Company. Indeed, much of that early contact was with fur traders. Fur would be exchanged for mainly cheap trinkets and bad spirit—of the alcoholic variety.

In 1797—about seven years before the famed Lewis and Clark expedition —David Thompson, one of the best-known land geographers of the time, visited the friendly Mandans and spent several weeks at the Knife River Village.

He reported that their agriculture included the growing of Indian corn, pumpkins, maize, beans and melons.

Alexander Henry, too, mentioned food in his journals, saying the women would pound parched corn into a meal and mix it with a little fat to form balls the size of hens' eggs. These would then be eaten as they were or gently fried.

Seven years *after* the Lewis and Clark expedition, in 1811, an Englishman called John Bradbury wrote of the Mandans' eating habits, saying they fed off dry buffalo meat and pounded corn.

Early descriptions of the Mandans include one from Maximilian, Prince of Weid, a German naturalist, soldier and author. He, too, stayed with the natives and said the Mandans were 'a vigorous, well-made race of people, rather above the middling stature, and very few of the men should be called short ...' He goes on:

> However, they are not so tall as the Manitaries [another term for Hidatsa]. Many of them are robust, broad shouldered, and muscular, while others are slender and small limbed. Their physiognomy is, in general, the same as that of most of the Missouri Indians, but their noses are not so long and arched as those of the Sioux, nor have they such high cheek bones. The nose of the Mandans and Manitaries is not broad—sometimes aquiline, or slightly curved, and quite often straight.

So here again is a description of the differences between the Mandan and the Sioux they probably interbred with after Madoc's famous journey.

Maximilian says the men were naked from the waist up, but wore a buffalo robe with the hair on the inside. It was decorated with human hair and coloured beads.

More evidence that the Mandans were a stationary people comes from Alexander Henry, who noticed on his travels that they were much more agricultural than even their neighbours, the Hidatsa:

> The Mandans are a stationary people who never leave their villages except to go hunting or on a war excursion. They are much more agricultural than their neighbors, the Big Bellies [Hidatsa], raising an

immense quantity of corn, beans, squash, tobacco, and sunflowers.

The Mandans' bull boats greatly resemble the famous Welsh coracle, which can still be seen on rivers such as the Teifi in West Wales. They were made with a green buffalo hide, which was lashed over a framework of bent poles made of willow or a similar, bendable, wood. They were very light and strong, and could carry fairly heavy loads in shallow water. One person could carry one quite easily, although they were often carried on a travois pulled by dogs or a horse.

They were used for navigation downstream or as a sort of ferryboat. However, the hide would eventually become soaked, so they couldn't remain in the water for long periods.

Back in the journals of Maximilian, I discovered interesting accounts of the Mandan marriage. The young man, he says, obtained the consent of the girl before approaching her father. If the father approved, a ritual of trading began. A number of horses—three to ten in number—were brought to the girl, who showed them to her father. He would then return an equal number of horses to the young suitor. This meant a careful guesstimate on the part of the young man, because he could not offer more horses than the girl's father could afford to exchange.

The courtship continued with the girl boiling corn each day and taking it to the young man's lodge. After a time, he would go to her lodge and spend the night with her, and the marriage was completed. The girl then had to enter into a life of hard work.

Maximilian says of the Mandan children that they weren't disciplined in the way most kids are:

> Everything is done to excite a spirit of Independence and self-will in the boys; if the mother speaks to one of them, he will very likely slap her face, or kick her, nay sometimes he will do the same to his father, who says, coolly, bowing his head, 'This boy will one day become a famous warrior.'

The three tribes and their lifestyle brought a lot of praise from travellers, geographers, fur traders and the like who made contact with them. They were admired for their simple way of life, sedentary, agricultural, proud, noble. They were living prosperously on the prairies—but because they had settled at a crossroads in the land-seeking, white man's empire, innumerable tragedies lay in store for the Mandan tribe. They would suffer more trouble from the Sioux, be devastated by smallpox and, even in this century, have their best land inundated by a white man's reservoir.

Perhaps the biggest and most ruinous events in the earlier history of the three tribes and their habitation of North Dakota were the smallpox epidemics. The second and more damaging epidemic struck the three tribes in June 1837 and spread very quickly. In order to escape its effects—or at least to minimize them—the Hidatsa spread along the Little Missouri. The Arikara hovered around Fort Clark. The Mandans, however, remained where they were, afraid to move out because of the marauding Sioux. The journals of Francis A. Chandon say that, by 30 September 1837, seven-eighths of the Mandans and half the Hidatsa and Arikara were wiped out.

At least one account says the Mandans were reduced from 1,800 in June to twenty-three men, forty women and sixty or seventy young people by the autumn of that year.

There had been an epidemic among the Mandans some seventy years before this. Their numbers had been cut by half and, faced with extinction, the thirty remaining families moved from the mouth of the Heart River, up north to Knife River. They built new lodges and lived partly with one and partly with the other of the two other tribes. However, they couldn't agree with the Arikara and by 1839 were living only with the Hidatsa.

Little by little, the three tribes claimed the river and reached Like-a-fish-hook Bend by 1844. The date of the permanent union of the three tribes is put at 1862, when they banded together against the Sioux.

The sky had changed since we'd moved out here to talk with Luther. The cold didn't seem to bother him too much. I could see that Cathy and the kids were beginning to feel it. But we were all fascinated still to hear this big Indian talk of his people and their friends the Hidatsa and the Arikara, and of the many rocks and boulders along the path of their history.

'Who's the chief now?' I asked.

'There are no more chiefs,' he said. 'When they all died off they weren't replaced. The last Mandan chief was named Sitting Crow. He died way back in the 1930s.'

I wondered if there was still animosity with the Sioux—considering that they'd conducted so many raids in the past.

'That all ended around 1880 to 1885,' said Luther. 'My

grandpa was still a warrior in 1880, 'cause they were still making raids on each other. My grandpa was a warrior with the US military forces for six years, too. He was a scout. Altogether he was a warrior for eighteen years.'

'Was he a full Mandan?'

'No, he had a little bit of Hidatsa in him, too. He had all those scars from sacrificing and fasting. He was about five ten and weighed about a hundred seventy-five pounds. Good-looking feller. And you could see the power in his eyes when he looked at you. You know, he was so powerful spiritually inside. But he never raised his voice, and he was always kind to me.'

Luther's face took on the look of one who can feel a story coming on.

'I remember once,' he said, 'he was gonna tell me a story. We loved stories. And I said to him in Hidatsa, "I know that story—go ahead and tell it." And he says, "You know that story?" And I says, "Yeah"—like a dummy, you know. And he said, "Well I don't need to tell you, do I?" And he never did, either. Boy, I begged him to tell me that story. He said, "You already know it." I never did that again, I can tell you.'

'What's the population of the reservation now?' I asked.

'Well, on the reservation there's about four, five thousand. But there are about that many off the reservation, living all over the United States. I used to live off the reservation. I was in the Army Air Corps in World War Two—an instructor on B-24s.'

'I didn't know Native Americans fought in the Second World War,' I said, showing my ignorance.

'Yeah, we did. But I really don't think we should have

been fighting wars for people that conquered us, and don't show us respect, you know. If they gave us recognition and treated us in a fair way . . .'

It was hard to disagree.

Chapter Nine

Under the stars

We had spent hours with Luther, after which he gave us his address and insisted we visit him on our return.

Cathy and I decided to look around with the kids. We crossed the Four Bears Bridge, which spans the Missouri, linking the separate parts of the reservation to each other. Without the bridge they'd be inaccessible to each other without a boat.

The view around us was spectacular, breathtaking. The rolling hills and never-ending prairie extended far beyond view.

Craig, Matthew and Stacey played on the banks of the Missouri, laughing and chasing each other. How uncomplicated life was for them! How simple their lives compared with those of the Native American children.

Four Bears Bridge over the Missouri.

The Indians, I reflected, were torn between American-ization and sticking with the culture and traditions that linked them with their past, their ancestors. This link now seemed to hang by a thread, celebrated only at certain times of the year. The older generations were desperately trying to hold on to the old ways, trying to make the younger generations see how important their roots are.

Night was drawing near, and we had decided to sleep under canvas. So, in the hired car that just didn't somehow belong in this magical land, we made our way west, deep into the prairie to spend our first night here, in the middle of Indian territory.

Although we'd camped in seclusion on our remote island the previous year, here it was different. We had the cold to contend with—but the experience was marvellous.

Here I was with my family, camped on one of the last frontiers, listening to the coyotes howling in the background, my mind mingling elements of the present and the past.

And I thought of Luther, and found myself thinking about the Welsh, and our treatment over the centuries by the English, how there were parallels between us and the Mandans (indeed, *all* Native American peoples as they struggled against white invaders to their lands). But to put that into perspective, let us look away from the American side of the connection for a moment, and turn our attention to Prince Madoc.

As I said at the beginning of Chapter One, my story begins more than eight hundred years ago, with Prince Madoc and his voyage to America. His is a story that has had historians arguing over the years—and I suppose they'll continue to do so.

Since coming back from the Cook islands, I had set to reading all I could about Madoc. His exploits in the New World are not a new subject, of course, and historians have dealt before with claims that he set foot there before Columbus. One man who tried to discredit the Madoc claim was John Evans. He was sent by Iolo Morganwg—an educated and erudite Glamorgan stonemason who founded the Gorsedd in 1792 (the Gorsedd is a society of Welsh bards, which still plays an integral part in the organization of the annual National Eisteddfod). Iolo Morganwg wanted to resolve the question of the Madoc–Mandan connection, and sent the twenty-one-year-old Evans to find out more.

However, soon after reaching America, Evans became a spy for the Spaniards, and subsequently claimed there were no Welsh Indians.

It has been a subject that is hard to shake off, though, and I believe Prince Madoc *did* sail to the New World. Why do I believe? Well, it's hard to live among the Mandan people and *not* believe, that's why. It's hard to talk to people like Luther Grinnell and Harry Sitting Bear and not believe a story about their people's past that is held true by that people itself.

And then there's a famous plaque in Alabama that seems to say without doubt that Madoc landed right there in Mobile Bay. I'll return to the plaque. But, first, back to Prince Madoc.

Madoc left his homeland of North Wales and took with him ten ships or more filled with dissatisfied Welsh people—all eager to begin their lives anew, away from strife and warfare. He had already been to the New World, having set off originally for Ireland and then venturing a good deal further. He had come back to assemble his group, with the intention of colonizing the land he'd discovered.

The King of the time was Henry II, who enjoyed exercising his control over Wales and Scotland. Although he had eight children, it was his son Richard Coeur de Lion (1157–99) who is known by most, made famous by the Robin Hood stories.

It is said that Prince Madoc set off on this particular, portentous voyage from Lundy Island in the Bristol Channel. He travelled through the Gulf of Mexico and it is presumed that some of the group decided to stay in South America, as there have been sightings of Welsh-speaking Indians there, too. Eventually, he landed in Mobile Bay, before moving up the Mississippi and settling in the interior of North America. A plaque erected by the Virginia Cavalier Chapter of the Daughters of the American Revolution at Mobile Bay, commemorates Madoc's landing in 1170. On top of the plaque the Welsh flag is illustrated, and the wording of the plaque is:

> In memory of Prince Madoc, a Welsh explorer, who landed on the shores of Mobile Bay in 1170 and left behind, with the Indians, the Welsh language.
> Authority is ~ Encyclopedia Americana copyright 1918 ~ Webster's Encyclopedia ~ Richard Hakluyt, 1552 to 1616, a Welsh Historian and Geographer ~ Ridpath's History of the World ~ ancient Roman coins found in Forts in Tenn. These Forts resemble the Forts of Wales of the 9th and 10th centuries and of the white Indians of the Tennessee and Missouri rivers.

The Richard Hakluyt mentioned on the plaque was educated at Westminster School and Christ Church College, Oxford. He also took holy orders, became prebendary of Bristol in 1586 and archdeacon of Westminster in 1586.

Hakluyt advocated the colonial school of thought and sea power—but it was merchant shipping rather than warships that he had in mind. He published a work called *Divers Voyages touching the Discovery of America* in 1582. This was intended to educate the reading public in the enterprise that Sir Humphrey Gilbert was about to embark on: the colonization of North America.

Gilbert (c.1539–83) was an English explorer who had a distinguished career as a soldier before leading an attempt to colonize the New World in 1578–79. It was unsuccessful. On a second voyage in 1583, the year of his death, he claimed Newfoundland for Elizabeth I. However, on the trip homeward, his ship foundered in a storm off Nova Scotia and he was lost.

Richard Hakluyt didn't give prominence to Gilbert's intentions, but the idea had obviously seized his own imagination, and he wanted to familiarize the reading public with the idea of colonization.

When he was in Paris in the 1580s, Hakluyt began work on the comprehensively titled *The principall Navigations, Voiages and Discoueries of the English nation made by Sea or over Land, in the most remote and farthest distant Quarters of the earth at any time within the compasse of these 1500 yeeres.*

Hakluyt, therefore, is quite an authority to cite.

Then there was Ridpath's *History of the World*, along with the Roman coins and the fort. All, in their way, chronicles of Madoc's journey—and, clearly, authority enough for the Daughters of the American Revolution.

Madoc's exploits are also mentioned in David Powel's *The Historie of Cambria* (1584). Powel and Hakluyt are the oldest of the printed sources still known to be in existence.

Another source is that of Pennsylvania-born George Catlin, in *Letters and Notes on the Manners, Customs and Condition of the North American Indians* (1841), in which he surmised that Madoc's expedition reached the upper Missouri River valley, and that its members were the ancestors of the Mandan Indians.

There is also a tradition of a 'white Indian' settlement at Louisville, Kentucky, and several seventeenth- and eighteenth-century reports were published about encounters by frontiersmen with Welsh-speaking Indians.

So I don't think there's any conclusive evidence to support the claims of those anthropologists who reject any idea of a pre-Columbian landing on the continent. The evidence, for me—and for the people I spoke to on the reservation—is just too great to be ignored, and nothing would please me more than to have the whole controversy opened up once again and held up to the scrutiny of scholars and non-scholars alike. (And, while you can hardly approach a British town without seeing the name of its 'twin town' on the sign as you enter, why not have a New Town–Somewhere-In-Wales twinning? New Town is the centre of Indian matters and such a link would help to keep the debate alive and foster new friendships, while offering opportunities for Welsh children to visit Native Americans and vice versa.)

Once Madoc had landed in America, his problem

would have been finding a suitable settlement for his people. I don't believe they ever did.

After making their way through the interior, they tried to settle by cultivating fields and establishing a fine and growing colony, but they were always forced to move from one site to another by savage tribes, leaving behind their very distinctive wigwams, built two feet or more in depth and about thirty or forty feet in diameter, and of circular shape. And it was the design of these wigwams that led many to believe that only a people advanced in the arts of civilization could build in such a way.

The villages the Welsh colonists built were surrounded by walls, which in some places reached twenty or thirty feet in height. However, these fortifications—built to protect—finally became a prison for Madoc's people as they were constantly besieged by savage and warlike natives. While many of the group died as provisions ran out, the remainder formed a friendship with the natives.

It's difficult to say exactly when, but the Welsh people amalgamated with the Indians at some point. The next generation of children would have been half-breeds, very likely despised by other tribes because of this. We see much the same sort of racism today—and half-castes get it from *both* sides. Human nature doesn't really change much!

The half-breeds, then, decided to form themselves into a group and moved off up country, where they settled and increased in number and strength. They became known as the Mandans.

The word 'Mandan' could have come from the Welsh word 'mandon', which in turn comes from the English word 'madder'. Madder is a herbaceous climbing plant

(*Rubia tinctorum*), which has yellowish flowers, and a red dye is made from it. These days you'll most likely find it in the form of a synthetic substitute, also called madder. The Welsh of old used this dye—in its natural form, of course—to decorate clothes. (While we're on the subject of etymology, I may as well throw in the fact that 'madder' comes from an Old English word, 'maedere'.)

Another thing the Mandans were known for was their pottery. They would mould vases and pots from black clay and bake them in kilns set in the sides of hills or under the bank of a river. According to visitors to the tribe, this was a craft carried out by no other Native American people.

The tribe also had a talent for making beautiful and lasting blue-glass beads, which they wore around their necks in great quantity. Just how they were made was a tribal secret—and it seems to have been a skill passed on by their Welsh forefathers.

It wasn't until Welsh immigrants arrived in large numbers in the New World that the presence of Welsh Indians could be confirmed—although there had been some unconfirmed reports by Spanish and English explorers.

But one of the most interesting stories concerns the Reverend Morgan Jones's experiences, which he relates in a letter written on 10 March 1686 to a Dr Thomas Lloyd of New York.

Jones gives one of the earliest accounts by a Welshman of contact with the Mandans. In his letter he tells how, when he was chaplain to the Governor of Virginia, he was sent to Carolina by ship, landing at a place called Oyster Point.

There were problems with provisions, and Jones's party had to travel back by land. Six of them struggled through wilderness and, when they reached Tuscarora country, the Indians took them prisoner. During their captivity the group learned through their interpreter, who had overheard a conversation among the natives, that they were going to be killed.

Jones exclaimed in despair—and in Welsh—'Have I escaped so many dangers, that I must now be knocked on the head like a dog?' On hearing the Welsh language spoken, the Indians' attitude mysteriously altered. I can only assume that either the Indians into whose hands he had fallen had some knowledge of the Mandans' tongue, or Mandans were among them. Whatever was the case, Mr Jones and his party were not put to death. Indeed, the group spent four months with the Indians, and no doubt many topics of conversation were covered. Jones preached to the natives about three times a week during his stay. When the party left the tribe, they were given the supplies they needed to return home.

In the letter—which eventually found its way to the Ashmolean Museum in Oxford—Jones claims he would take any Welshman, or others, to the country to prove the veracity of his story. However, there's no evidence that his claims were ever followed up.

Another report of Welsh Indians came from a French explorer, Verendrye, whom Luther was telling us about when we visited him in New Town. He said the Mandans' mode of living was unlike that of any other Indian tribe he'd ever met. He was able to confirm that they had fair skin, as others had said, and he was sure they must have descended from European forebears. Their villages were laid out in streets, he wrote, and these were kept very clean. Their lodges, or wigwams, were made of logs and covered with earth, and they were circular. They lived not so much by hunting as off the land, growing corn, fruit and vegetables.

Verendrye also vouched for their cooking—it would do justice to any European table, he wrote. And that's from a Frenchman, whose fellow countrymen always seem to believe they're in the culinary ascendant!

Verendrye was so excited by what he'd discovered that he left behind two men to learn the Mandan language.

Of all the men who spent time with the Mandans, the one who inspires me most is George Catlin, who was born in Pennsylvania in 1796—one of fourteen children. Like me, he took an early interest in American Indian life. He became a lawyer, but practised for only two years before giving it up to become a portrait painter. In 1831, he visited the American Indians and studied their lifestyles: languages, customs, arts and artefacts, appearance, tools and so on.

Altogether he spent seven years with them, making many notes and sketches. During this time he spent a long period with the Mandans, and his paintings of the Mandan people, especially the women, showed how they differed from other tribes, with their high brows and blue eyes.

Catlin says of the Mandan canoes that they were different from those of other tribes—almost round in shape (just like the Welsh coracle, in fact).

Catlin was convinced the first time he set eyes on them that the Mandan people were a mixture of native North American and some other race.

In his book *North American Indians*, he wrote:

> The Mandans are certainly a very interesting and pleasing people, in their personal appearance and manners, differing in many respects, both in looks and customs, from all other tribes I have seen ...
>
> So forcibly have I been struck with the peculiar ease and elegance of these people, together with the diversity of complexions and various colours of their hair and eyes, the singularity of their language and their peculiar customs, that I am convinced that they have sprung from origin other than that of the other North American tribes.

He goes on to describe some linguistic similarities between the Mandan tongue and Welsh. Here are a few of them.

ENGLISH	MANDAN	WELSH	WELSH PRONUNCIATION
I/me	me	mi	me
no	megosh	nagoes	nagoiss
head	pan	pen	pen
great	maho	mawr	maoor

Sir Walter Raleigh (c.1552–1618—who organized several voyages of exploration and colonization to the Americas—produces some evidence of Indian words that corresponded with Welsh words of the same meaning. He claims some colonists were greeted by Indians shouting words such as '*iach*' and '*yachi tha*'. '*Iach*' means 'healthy', and '*iechyd*' means 'health' itself. When non-speakers of Welsh take the mickey with the phrase 'yacky dah!', they're really saying (although often don't realize it) '*iechyd da!*', which means 'cheers!' or (literally) 'good health!'.

Welsh migration to America began in earnest in the seventeenth century. One interesting link with the Madoc story concerns the arrival of the Merrick brothers in Massachusetts in 1636. They had sailed from Bristol and were descendants of Meyrick ap Llewellyn, whose father, Llewellyn ap Heylin, fought at Bosworth on the side of Henry Tudor, and was, through the Heylins of Bodorgan, a reputed descendant of Madoc. The Merrick crest is still to be found on colonial silverware in the USA.

In the time leading up to the Declaration of Independence on 4 July 1776, Welsh influence on American affairs was strong. Among the generals of the revolution were John Cadwaladr, Andrew Lewis, Morgan Lewis, Daniel Morgan, James Thomas, John Thomas and Joseph Williams—Welshmen all. Thomas Jefferson (1743–1826)—who was the principal drafter of the Declaration of Independence and played a key role in the War of Independence (1775–83)—had ancestors in Snowdonia. Among the signatories to the Declaration were men of Welsh origin, among them William Williams, Lewis Morris and Francis Lewis. Lewis was a native of Llandaff, and sat as a member of the Committee of One Hundred. His son, Morgan Lewis, became Governor of New York in 1804.

The majority of Welsh migrants were from remote villages, and sought similar territory once in America by settling in Indiana, Illinois, Wisconsin and Minnesota. This shows how people on the move, while no doubt enthusiastic about the novelty of a new life, new horizons, will eventually seek what is most comfortable for them: the familiar.

It almost seemed that a Welsh love of the New World was foretold by Madoc's journey. And, in the case of the Mandans, many things the Welsh people had done were carried on in their own American traditions: coracles, a way of building homes, jewellery, other artefacts such as beads and pottery.

The more I read about the Mandans, the more convinced I become that they are the descendants of Madoc and his party of fellow travellers.

Chapter Ten

Words

That first night camping on the prairie was an experience I'll never forget. The sounds of the animals in the night were exhilarating: enjoyable and just a little frightening. But the below-minus temperature wasn't easy to contend with. We huddled together for warmth in our small tent, having donned as many clothes as would be comfortable, and eventually we even managed to fall asleep.

In the morning the temperature had risen to about five degrees, but it felt just as cold. However, it was bright and clear and invigorating.

We packed away our things, got everything into the hired car and set off back to the Tribal Administration Center. We hoped we'd be able to see Ed Lone Fight—the guy who had, after all, sent us the letter inviting us to come.

'Dad,' Matthew pestered as we drove back, 'when are we going to ride some horses?'

'Not sure yet, Math,' I told him. 'We'll try to get something arranged soon.'

'Will I have to go on a horse with you, Mammy?' Stacey asked with a little apprehension.

'Let's just wait and see what we can sort out,' her mam said.

'OK, Mam. I hope I can, though.'

Cathy laughed.

We did get to see Ed Lone Fight. He's the Tribal Programs Manager, and it was a brief meeting, because he's a very busy man. It's not uncommon for him to be dashing off to Washington to discuss funding for education, for health programmes or other developments on the reservation. Despite his numerous commitments and duties he still managed to arrange for us to go riding in the Bad Lands. He also introduced us to Harry Sitting Bear, a huge man whose size matches his name—although that's where any ursine resemblance ends. And he told us we should visit Doris McGrady, the local school principal, who had put her telephone number on the letter Ed had sent to us—intrigued by our research and wishing to meet us.

Ed Lone Fight breaks from his hectic schedule to chat with visitors from Wales.

Harry is a gentle giant, a bespectacled man with his ample grey-black hair tied behind his head, his large face at once welcoming, intelligent and radiating tranquillity.

Harry offered to show us an earth lodge, and we jumped at the chance to see one. These lodges aren't used any more by the natives. Nowadays the Mandans live in cabin-style houses.

I was quite taken aback by the size of the earth lodge. It was about eight foot high and fifteen foot wide—and the one we were looking at, according to Harry, was quite small compared with the original Mandan and Hidatsa dwellings.

Then Matthew piped up excitedly: 'Dad, I've seen houses like this—on one of my trips with the school.'

I was stunned. I had never thought to make any comparison between Welsh and Native American architecture. I think what Luther had said about the similarity had washed over all the other information we were having to assimilate, and it hit me now what he'd said, 'That looks like a Celtic-type thing of old, you know.'

'Where did you see that, Math?' I asked.

'I, um, I think it was Castell Henllys . . . I'm not sure.' This was a reference to a reconstructed Iron Age village near Cardigan in west Wales. Matthew had been there on a school trip, in common with thousands of schoolkids. He'd obviously spotted a similarity straight away, and, although we didn't know it then, before long we'd be showing Harry Sitting Bear the Celtic constructions when he came to Wales to visit.

I turned to Harry. 'Do you think the Mandans are an amalgamation of Native Americans and Welsh people of centuries ago?' I asked him.

'My great-grandfather on my mother's side was Crow Flies High,' Harry said. 'He had wavy hair and fair skin, and I've heard that the Mandan language is different to that of other tribes.'

I showed him some words in Mandan—the ones I'd seen compared to Welsh words—and asked him if they were correct.

'"*Maho Peneta*"—"the Great Spirit",' I said, 'is that correct?'

'Yes, that's correct,' he said.

I showed him a list of Welsh and Mandan words, and asked him if they were significantly similar.

'Most of them are,' he said. 'The Mandan and Welsh languages are very similar,' said Harry, showing some surprise.

'Do many native Mandans believe in the Madoc legend?' I asked.

'There could be truth in it,' he said. 'Because when Lewis and Clark came they took a Mandan back with them called Big White—and he was like those ones I told you about: fair-skinned and blue-eyed. I mentioned that my great-grandfather, Crow Flies High, had wavy hair and fair skin—well, his son, my grandfather, had blue eyes; my cousin when he was young had yellow hair, like that'—pointing to Matthew —'but now his hair is darker. So, somewhere, those traits were introduced into the tribe.'

We left the site of the earth lodge and moved up on to a hillside that gave us a spectacular view over the south side of the reservation. I asked Harry to tell us more about his great-grandfather, Crow Flies High.

'My great-grandfather didn't like what was going on

on the reservation,' Harry began. 'There was alcohol, steamboats and gambling. The natives started to lose their Indian ways.

'So, in 1869, Crow Flies High left with his people and went north—about a hundred and eighty five of them in all. They consisted of both Mandan and Hidatsa, and they stayed around the Buford and Billings area, which is near Montana. They stayed out there for twenty-five years, before being ordered by the military to leave the area and return to the reservation.

'They were made to walk the whole way, during the month of March, when the weather was cold. Although they agreed to return to Little Knife River, they refused to agree with conditions of settlements on the individual plots, so in 1894 they eventually settled in the Shell Creek Area.

'My great-grandfather died just four years later.' Harry gave a little chuckle. 'I bet those people could tell a story or two,' he said. 'The experiences they had endured during their lives.'

He smiled and put an arm on my shoulder.

'Tony,' he said, 'I think you were born five hundred years too late.'

'You're not the only one to say that,' Cathy piped up. She had really taken to North Dakota and the reservation. She felt totally at ease with the people and the surroundings. Although she had enjoyed island life to some extent, she seemed to prefer life here.

'Tony,' said Harry as we walked, 'I want you and the family to meet some Mandans. First I will introduce you to Bernice. She's an old lady who will talk to you about her past.'

Harry took us to Bernice's home. She lived in a wooden cabin containing several apartments, specially built for elderly people on the reservation. It was Bernice's seventy-fifth birthday and luckily we had brought gifts from Wales, so we were able to give her a teatowel depicting a Welsh woman playing a harp, surrounded by the days and months printed in Welsh.

We all shuffled into her unit. There wasn't much room in it. There were three rooms in all: a bedroom, a bathroom and the room in which we stood, looking a little self-conscious. I was thinking how poky it looked compared with the spacious earth lodges the people had lived in long ago.

Harry introduced us: 'Cathy, Tony, this is my mom—not my natural mom, but by mom's sister. My mother died, so my auntie is now my mom.'

'Yes,' Bernice replied. 'And he is my son now. That is our way.'

'Is that the way it's always been?' I asked.

'Yes,' she said, 'always. Please sit down.'

Harry excused himself. 'I have to get back to the administration centre,' he said. 'Meet me back there when you've finished here.' And with that he was gone.

Bernice appraised us all with wise old eyes. I didn't really know how to start, so I came straight to the point: 'Do you mind if we ask you some questions?'

'No,' she said, 'I don't mind. You can ask questions.'

'Do you remember much of the old ways?' I asked.

'Yes. I remember when I was eight years old. I lived with my grandmother. She taught me many things. Her language was Mandan—that's all she talked. She was a basket weaver and a porcupine-quill worker. She worked with porcupine quills, dying them in different colours. You snip off both sides of a wide flat quill and then you sew them and make pretty designs and fancy work.'

Bernice told us about her tribe's agricultural traditions. 'Some tribes call us the Corn People,' she said, 'because we are agriculture people. We planted gardens and we didn't go anywhere, not like nomads. We didn't do that. We stayed right here along the Missouri river.'

'We saw an earth lodge,' I said. 'You don't live in those any more.'

'Not for a long time now. They were sturdy. We don't move, so we would stay in the village—not like the Sioux. They would have a small shelter and then move on. We would stay where we were. We would have gardens and store everything in the earth lodge—even our horses and our dogs were inside. All you can see from the outside is the lodge.'

'Did you marry a Mandan?' I asked.

'I married *Victor* Mandan when I was nineteen.' She seemed to pause a while, waiting for the coincidence of the name to sink in. We looked at each other, and Bernice smiled. 'I had six children,' she resumed, 'five boys. They went to Vietnam in the war, and they all came back. Only two got wounded.

'And I have a daughter. When a young girl gets married her firstborn is given to the grandparents—well, not given exactly, but the grandparents take it, whether it's a boy or a girl. And they will teach this child.'

'Is that just the Mandans?'

'I'm just speaking for the Mandans,' she said. 'The grandparents will then raise this child. I was the oldest, so Grandma and Grandpa took me. Mama came to stay with us, but it was always Grandma and Grandpa I had to listen to.

'Grandma would teach me: "Women don't do this, women don't do that, women have to do this . . ." But it was different for the boys. I had about six cousins—boys. One was called the Lone Bear. Grandpa would teach them games, teach them work outside and teach them how to fish and hunt, and they would have to be real good with arrows.

'We would have games, too—the girls. In fact, I used to have a little ball, decorated with quillwork. It was really pretty. And we'd have a little cane, too. We'd bounce that ball right here on our feet. I used to have a basket and it had some rocks in it. Today I think they were gold, because they were kinda brownish in colour, and when you scraped them with something sharp they were really shiny.'

'So you could have been playing with some valuable gold?' I asked.

'Yeah. I think it must have been. And we never knew it. But we were not worried about money. We lived without money. We survived off the land. The earth would give to us. We would plant and we'd get berries and we would get animals to eat. We had the river and the springs from the ground. There was no need of money.'

'Were both your grandparents Mandan?' Cathy asked.

'Yes, yes they were.'

'And what about your parents?'

My father and mother are both Mandan. My father was a big man.'

I thought of Luther Grinnell, and told her about him—how big he was.

'Oh, yeah, but he's skinny. My dad was big, broad.'

I couldn't stifle my urge to smile, and Bernice seemed to know what I was thinking. Luther's one helluva big guy, so her dad must have been a giant.

'And Luther's half white,' she added, as if this somehow gave her dad the edge over Luther. But I don't think there was any malice in her comparison: just observation.

'Did your grandparents ever tell you stories of their past?' I asked her.

'My grandma told me of when they fetched big stacks of blankets, which all the Indians liked because they were not like the robes they had. The buffalo robes they had were heavy.

'Anyhow, these blankets were all from dead people—soldiers. They were infested with smallpox, and they gave these to the Indians.' She was bearing out the story Luther had told us the previous day.

'Was that on purpose?' I asked.

Bernice paused before she spoke, then she said, 'Just to be mean. And many, many died from that smallpox. A whole earth lodge would be infected with that disease. Sometimes they would all die together.'

'And your grandmother remembered all this?' Cathy asked her.

'Yes. She said those steamboats would come up, and her and her sister, they would sit there, and the soldiers, they would give out things. My grandmother watched. Then they would look for the little kids. They would give them sticks of candy, which was made from molasses. It's sweet, like syrup, but not as good. She said they would pat the kids' heads and say "nice *pupusy*", but she thought they were saying "*ti pupusy*", which means spotted prairie

99

dog. And all along they were saying "pretty *pupusy*". They didn't understand each other.

'Anyhow, the Mandans called the soldiers "*wasinahorosh*", which means "those generous people are coming". And the Hidatsa group, when they heard the Mandans saying that, they didn't know what they were, so they called them *mashi*. Today all the white people are known as *mashi*. The white people linked us to the Sioux tribe, because the Sioux language is similar to ours. For "water" the Sioux say "*mahini*", and the Mandans say "*mahimi*".'

'Going back to what the soldiers did,' I said, 'I suppose it was nothing less than criminal.'

'They demolished the people. They wanted the land. We have been pushed around so many times. If you go by Riversdale and Garrison, and try to cross the water, you will see how big the water is. It's just like a big sea. It's terrible. We just have very little land. We all had gardens—now we don't have gardens. They gave us canned goods—canned food to eat all the time, which isn't good for us. Many natives are diabetic. We didn't have proper food. The river on both sides used to be thick with trees—fruit trees and everything.'

'What happened to the trees?' Cathy asked.

'The army engineers came and cut all the wood off. We didn't have anything,' said Bernice, 'not even a stick for firewood. They cut all the trees, then they flooded the area. They made us all move up to higher ground. Now the whole land is all flooded.'

I asked Bernice, 'We were told that even today the land is being taken from the natives. Is that right?'

'Yes. They're still taking it. We don't have much left now.'

'I thought that this was quite a big reservation.'

'No, it isn't. It's just a little compared to what it used to be,' she said.

'Is the land on the reservation good?'

'The land is good here. We have coal and oil. We have oil on our land. We've had wells built up, and our coal is lignite coal. That's the best kind.'

'But can the American government still take the land off you if they want to?'

'Yeah,' she said with a sigh. 'The President of the United States has the authority. He will listen to the white man's voice, but he will not listen to us.'

Cathy had become quite worked up by this time, and you could hear a vicarious resentment in her voice. 'But it's your land, though,' she said, hardly believing all that she'd just heard. 'All of it!'

'It's our land,' said Bernice, 'but we have no voice. We can't do anything. I am here now but I belong across the river.'

'If your land is across the river,' asked Cathy, 'can't you go back there?'

'No,' said Bernice bitterly. 'We had horses and cattle. Now we don't have anything. They brought the white people's cattle in and the ranchers lease our land. Once a year we get payment. I think it's five or ten cents an acre they lease it for.'

Bernice was not a lover of the White America, it seemed. She paused a moment in her story, seeming to cast her mind around for more evidence.

'When my grandmother was living, when any white people—a minister or doctor or anybody—came toward our cabin, she would tell me to hide. Then she would take a big knife that she had and tell whoever it was that there's nobody here, and you'll have to kill me before you do anything. That's why I never went to school until she died. That was when I was eight.

'Then they took me to school. They cut my braids off—cut my hair just straight across. Now in our Indian beliefs, if your husband or brother dies in war, *that's* when you have the right to cut your hair off. But they did that to us.'

'Who cut your hair?' asked Cathy.

'The schoolteachers. And if we spoke our language we got punished or they would starve us. That's why a lot of the younger people don't speak the language today.'

I thought of a parallel with my own land.

'The English did the same thing to us Welsh many years ago,' I said. 'They tried to stop us using the Welsh language. Today only a minority speak Welsh.'

'Well, one thing we keep, I tell you—and that's our religion. Although they baptized us in their churches, we keep our religion. What Grandma and Grandpa teach us, we keep in here.' And she touched her chest. 'What they teach us is instilled in our hearts. It doesn't go away. And today my sons have a Sun Dance every summer. It would be nice if you could stay for the summer and watch the Sun Dance.'

'What *is* the Sun Dance?' I asked Bernice.

'It's our religion. It's our prayers. Menfolk will go out on a high hill and fast for four days and four nights. There's no food, no water: just prayers and offering of smoke to the Great Spirit. Then, after four days, they come down and they go in a sweat lodge for purification. After that they dance to the sun, and you can hear their songs.'

'What do the women do?' Cathy asked.

'They'll help with the cooking. Some will dance, too.'

After hearing of Luther's grandfather earlier, I was keen to hear of others and it was fascinating to be talking to someone who had spoken to those who had lived during the last century. So I asked Bernice what her own grandfather was like.

'When my grandfather spoke, we had to listen, because he always said, "Hear me now while my voice is here; tomorrow you may not hear my voice."

'His Indian name meant "like a horse",' she said, 'a white horse that ran swiftly. My grandfather used to tell us about the white men who had the same religion as us, all over the world, but would make fun of us when we went out to fast. But if they opened their minds more, he said, they would see that Abraham went fasting. Moses went fasting—he went up on a big mountain and when he came down he was changed. He had a vision. That's what we do today. Look at Jesus—he fasted forty days and forty nights, and when he came back he was changed. So we *do* fast, we *do* have visions, and we're taught different things. And that's something we don't give up.'

Bernice had been a great help, and we'd enjoyed listening to her. We decided it was time to leave her to her thoughts. We thanked her and kissed her on both cheeks.

'You're welcome,' she said. 'I enjoy talking about the past.' She gave me a warm smile, then turned her attention to Cathy and the children. She kissed them all before saying, 'You must all try to come back. You will be very welcome.'

Chapter Eleven

Horse sense and animal magic

After our fascinating couple of hours with Bernice, we all had a refreshing night's sleep and awoke with horse riding on our minds. This was the day we'd promised the kids they'd get into the saddle at last.

But first we had a visit to make. This time to the principal of the local school, Doris McGrady. With a name like McGrady, we didn't know what to expect—but Doris, we'd been told, was part native (the other part being Irish, on her father's side). Doris had actually asked to meet us and she was to supply us with some remarkable linguistic evidence for the Madoc theory.

Doris is in her forties —a warm, friendly, petite woman, very relaxed. She ushered us into her cosy home and immediately made us feel welcome. Cooking smells wafted in from the kitchen, adding to the feeling of warmth and homeliness.

She was excited about our research. The Madoc story had intrigued her since childhood, when her father would talk of Madoc and his followers, and of their amalgamation with the Indians.

'Do you think there *is* a connection?' was my first question, after we'd got the formalities out of the way.

'Oh, yes,' she said. 'It seems that the Mandan language doesn't appear to be linguistically connected to other tribes. For instance, if you look at the linguistic divisions, you have a whole group of tribes speaking a Sioux-based language. The Mandan doesn't fit into most of those categories. It's similar'—I thought of what Bernice had told us about '*mahini*' and '*mahini*'—'but it doesn't fit very well. I imagine that whatever language they spoke before the Welsh influence certainly is there, and so there is just enough of it to connect it to one of the major language stocks. But not very much. The connections are very scattered. It really doesn't fit. And I think that's the Welsh influence that has changed it.'

'On the map west of here there's a place called Madoc,' I said. 'Where does that come from?'

'I don't know, but I've often wondered about that. I've always known about this name, because my father and I used to talk of this a lot—the connection between the Welsh and the Mandans—and he told me about that town, but I never knew where that name came from.' Returning to the Mandan people, Doris continued, 'You know, everything—from the physical appearance to the agriculture, the commerce, the way the structures were made—everything is similar to the Welsh.'

I mentioned the similarities noticed by explorers such as Lewis and Clark.

'You know, I think it's ironic,' she said, suddenly, as though a new thought had hit her, 'that not only is the Mandan language disappearing, but so is the Welsh.'

Well, maybe not disappearing, I thought, but certainly in a minority. After all, we've had the Welsh Language Board for a few years now, regulating what must be expressed in both English and Welsh, but there are many who say this is not enough. Vocal among them, of course, is the Welsh Language Society, or Cymdeithas yr Iaith Gymraeg.

'We were talking to a lady yesterday, Bernice,' I told Doris. 'It was her seventh-fifth birthday. She told us she actually preferred the past. She was telling us about the earth lodges—that they were more comfortable than what she's living in now.'

'That's true,' said Doris.

'Everything's changing now,' I said. 'Everything's so modern, and yet people seem to crave for the past.'

'That's true also. Has that happened to the Welsh people? Are they less healthy for the same reason?'

'I think in Wales people tend to eat a lot of fat foods and there's a lot of heart trouble,' I said, racking my brains for the statistics that say Welsh men are especially prone to heart disease.

'Ah, heart problems,' Doris repeated. 'That's exactly what's occurring here with the Indians.'

'I've noticed there are a lot of light-skinned natives,' I offered.

'The light skin and light eyes of the Mandan people has through all of history—since contact was made—surprised those who met them,' she said.

'This is why we think there is a strong link,' I said, 'because there was a Madoc who is a legend in Wales. Ships went missing during the reign of Henry the Second. Cathy and I think Madoc took them and left Wales from Lundy Island, and ended up in Mobile Bay. There's a plaque there, commemorating the landing in 1170. He disappeared with his people and a few hundred years later explorers found the Mandans, and they had this language, so to me there has got to be a link.'

'I'm just certain of it,' said Doris. 'Once in a while you read something that reaffirms it.'

Cathy and I could see that the children were beginning to get restless, so we decided to put our Madoc conversation on hold.

'Are you kids hungry?' asked Doris.

They looked at one another before chorusing, 'Yes!'

It wasn't surprising. We hadn't eaten for a few hours, and the aroma that had been wafting in from the kitchen was enough to make anyone want food.

'OK,' she said, 'let's go eat.'

We all sat around the six-seater table, already laid, which stood between the sitting room and kitchen. Doris went to the small, fitted and well-equipped kitchen and removed a large pot from the oven. She brought it over and placed it in the centre of the table. Then she dished out a bowl apiece of the pot's contents: beef stew. The kids cleared their plates quickly.

It wasn't until our second helping that I mentioned our plans to go horse riding.

'If you're planning to ride over the Bad Lands you should visit my Uncle. He can speak the Mandan dialect. And that beef stew will be good for you.'

We thanked Doris and, after writing down the address of her uncle, Clyde Baker, headed south.

Ed Lone Fight had given us the name and directions of a ranch where we could find horses. He'd even telephoned the ranch for us, so we were expected.

The ranch was at Killdeer, south of New Town. Cathy and I were a little apprehensive. None of us had ever ridden a horse before—unless you count Cathy's experience on a donkey during a school outing. It always looks so easy and natural when you see people on television—especially those who use the horse for transport. I've sat through many a Western and other films that show people in the Great Outdoors, and the ease with which they control the animal while remaining firmly—and *comfortably*—in the saddle never ceases to amaze me.

When the kids had first clamoured for horse riding, and we'd said yes, I suppose I hadn't really thought about it too deeply. If I had I might have had second thoughts.

So Cathy and I were a little apprehensive. And yet it would be a journey in time for me. Something of the old Wild West, I suppose. It appealed to the romantic in me.

The children were, of course, excited—and that's putting it mildly. It was about a hundred and twenty miles to Killdeer and they talked non-stop all the way about what they planned to do once they were on their horses.

We were met at the ranch by Steve—looking the part in denims, cowboy hat and boots. Soon, we were looking at six beautifully groomed horses. Steve, sounding as well like someone straight out of a Western movie, took Stacey to a large brown animal. 'Let me introduce you to Honda,' he told her. She turned to us and gave a puzzled look. But Steve sensed her anxiety. 'You'll be OK,' he said. 'Honda'll take good care of you. He's the best we got.'

And with that he lifted her gently into the saddle. 'What's your name?' he asked her.

'Stacey,' came the whispered reply.

'Hey, now, you don't have to be so nervous,' he said. But Stacey just sat stiffly upright in the saddle, which Steve found amusing. However, he eased her nerves with the consummate skill of a doctor telling a patient he was about to have his head removed but everything would be just fine. Really it would.

'See this in front of you, Stacey?' he said. 'It's called the horn. You hold on to it with your left hand, see? Like this.'

Stacey silently followed his instructions, visibly calming as she did so.

'With your right hand,' said Steve, 'you hold the reins. Yup, that's right. But don't hold them too tight, now. Leave a little slack. And if you want to stop Honda just pull the reins back gently and say, "Whoa, Honda". And he'll listen to you. OK?'

After he'd patiently shown Stacey the rudiments of equine manipulation, it was Matthew's turn. And Matthew needed no cajoling. He'd waited long and patiently for this adventure, and now his time had arrived.

His horse was called Trigger. Whether Trigger was as well trained as Roy Rogers's horse of the same name remained to be seen. Trigger was a beautiful golden colour—almost matching Matthew's hair.

Steve helped him into the saddle, beaming at us—a small smile first, quickly spreading into a grin. He seemed so pleased with himself.

It was Craig's turn. He was just as eager as Matthew (although, being the eldest, he probably thought it wouldn't be the done thing to show *too* much childlike enthusiasm). Craig was being helped into the saddle of a horse called Doc.

Then Honda—Stacey's mount—decided to make a move. Cathy drew in a breath and held it, her face contorting into something resembling a wince. But her concern was short-lived: Stacey took complete control.

'Whoa, Honda, whoa!' she shouted, entering into the spirit of things with unbounded joy. Honda came to an immediate stop as Stacey pulled on the reins.

'Hey, that's very good, Stacey,' Steve told her, as he ushered Cathy to her horse. Craig and Matthew were by now looking quite relaxed on their mounts—but Cathy, on Molly, was just a little uneasy. Molly had a mind of her own, wandering in all directions. I was reminded of an amusing scene during a stay on our Island when Cathy was adrift in a canoe. It was moving this way and that in the lagoon, and Cathy was unable to control it. Molly was Cathy's dry-land canoe.

I was on Lincoln, who seemed placid enough. All the horses except Trigger—Matthew's horse—were brown of one shade or another. I'm sure there are technical terms for horse colours, but I don't know them.

Food and other belongings were stored in the saddlebags and we set off. Steve was in the lead, while I brought up the rear. Stacey was close behind Steve, then Cathy, who now seemed to have reached a working arrangement with Molly, and the boys were behind her.

Mother and daughter in the saddle:
Cathy on Molly and Stacey on Honda.

Cathy tried to take some photographs as we began our journey—but Molly seemed to have other ideas. Whether it was the click and whirr of the camera or the fact that Cathy had to take her hands off the reins I don't know, but Molly decided to wander hither and thither and just didn't want to know.

The scenery that confronted us was out of this world. Here was North Dakota spreading out in front of us, behind us and to either side. Vastness induces an excitement in most of us, and this panorama was no exception. Dakota is beautiful country. Forest covers only about one per cent of the land, and trees are to be found mainly near river valleys—oak, ash and cottonwood mostly. There's small red cedar in the Bad Lands, and an abundance of wild flowers grow on the prairie. Then there are several varieties of grass—grama, blue stem, wheat grass—all decorating a terrain speckled with thousands of prairie marshes.

At one time herds of bison roamed free all over the prairies of the West. Nowadays they're to be found mainly in parks such as the Theodore Roosevelt National Park (which accommodates the Bad Lands), along with elk, antelope, deer, bighorn sheep and wild horses. The national park is split into two units called the North and South, spanning more than 70,000 acres. The rugged terrain and vast open spaces are a romantic's dream—a link with those days of Sitting Bull, General Custer, Lewis and Clark, Theodore Roosevelt, Sakakawea and other legendary figures.

The famous buttes of the Bad Lands are nothing short of spectacular—ranging in colour from a sort of putty yellow to blazing reds.

Although I'm not a birdwatcher, I can understand why people who are go to North Dakota. Twitchers—or birders, as the Americans call them—find it a paradise, I'm sure, with more than 350 species of songbird, shorebird, wading bird, bird of prey, nesting waterfowl. Names such as western grebe, ferrunginous hawk, Hungarian partridge, sharp-tailed grouse, piping plover, upland sandpiper, Franklin's gull, Sprague's pipit, marbled godwit and chestnut-collared longspur adorn the tourism literature entreating people to sample the ornithological delights.

Then there are the National Grasslands: Sheyenne and Little Missouri. Sheyenne National Grassland is in the southeastern part of the state, and is North Dakota's only stronghold for the greater prairie chicken. In the spring the ardent bird-watcher can see migratory songbirds here, such as vireos, meadowlarks, orioles, sparrows and warblers.

Little Missouri National Grassland covers 1.2 million acres of prairie and Bad Lands habitats in western North Dakota. Here can be seen mule deer, white-tailed deer, prairie dogs and golden eagles. And they're just a few of the pleasures that await the wildlife enthusiast.

And if I'm starting to sound like a travel agent's glossy literature, it's because I was so moved by the land I was in that if I could write poetry I'd have filled several volumes by now!

The State Forests—Homen and Turtle Mountain—are no less interesting. Here can be found aspen, bur oak, green ash and balsam poplar, which tend to be the home of moose, white-tailed deer, ducks, ruffed grouse and many small animals. No less a variety of birds and animals is to be found in Turtle Mountain State Forest where, again, oak and aspen are in abundance.

I could go on about the wild beauty and rugged magic of the place —but I won't. Suffice it to say that my trip through the Bad Lands was an experience neither I nor Cathy will forget in a hurry. And it was an education for our three children that I wish all kids could experience.

As we rode, I couldn't help but reflect on how lucky we were.

'Hold on tight, kids!' Cathy shouted. Steve had guided us over a small trail, and a little to our left was a forty-foot drop. I didn't need her to caution me: Lincoln was already looking over the drop, and I prayed he wasn't feeling suicidal. I gently stroked his neck and told him that perhaps it wouldn't be a good idea to jump.

As we rode on, the gap between me and the others began to widen as I took in the beauty of the Bad Lands, with its stimulating topography, strange land forms, rocks produced by layers of sandstone, mudstone and black lignite coal.

I nudged Lincoln with my heel, and he went into a canter. I held on —hoping for the best, but I was not at all convinced I'd remain in the saddle for the entire ride. I managed to catch up with Cathy and we rode side by side.

Soon I was back into the rhythm of the ride until Steve announced—as casually is if he were commenting on the weather—that we were about to reach a small ravine, '. . . and your horses may want to jump it.'

At this point I began to feel just a little alarmed. Not only had I not ridden before but here we were about to leap to our deaths and be battered to a pulp—along with our horses—on a million jagged rocks thousands of feet below.

'. . . so hang on to the reins tightly.' Steve's voice seemed miles away. All I could think of was this great fissure in the landscape and that I was about to tumble into it.

'What about Stac—' But Cathy's words were cut short as Stacey, now following Steve's example, nudged her horse's side and she was away. We all followed suit. Cathy and I passed Matthew and Craig, who were both grinning from ear to ear, clearly looking forward to the jump ahead. I think I warmed to the idea as the excitement grew. We stopped at a bank. There was a slope. At the bottom lay this two-foot ravine that had worried me so. It was followed by quite a steep stony hill on the other side. We held our breath. Stacey made her way down the slope. In one swift move her horse had cleared the water in the small ravine and I began mentally to kick myself for my blind panic of just a few short moments before.

Stacey laughed out loud as her horse began to make its way up the slope at the other side. She was obviously enjoying every second of it.

The boys were next—again, swift, smooth, effortless movements carrying them over. Cathy's jump was similar.

Then it was my turn. I continued the descent towards the water, waiting for the exhilarating sensation of the jump. The water came closer. Lincoln cantered on. I held my breath. I closed my eyes.

Nothing happened.

Lincoln had decided he'd prefer to *walk* through the water.

'You darn critter,' I wanted to say in my best John

Wayne drawl. But I kept my mouth shut and pretended that I had displayed such absolute control over the horse that his decision to saunter through the water had been my own choice all along. I don't think Steve was fooled by my nonchalance, however. Come to that, Cathy and the kids were giving me funny looks, too.

A few hours passed. I had a sore bum, and I suspected Cathy and the kids did, too, but I didn't think it prudent to ask. Cathy rode alongside Stacey, who seemed to be engaged in a deep conversation with Honda, telling him how she wanted to take him home to Wales. She had clearly made a friend.

I rode with the boys. 'When are we going to gallop?' Craig asked—yet again. He had been asking this for the past hour and a half. I changed the subject. I wasn't *quite* ready for that. Not just yet.

We came to a stop near an escarpment, where there was grass for the horses to graze.

'I wish David was here,' Craig muttered as he dismounted. David and Craig had been through primary school together and David had lived opposite us in Swansea. He was one of thirteen children. His parents had eventually got their wish to move back to their native Ireland—but David was missing his old friends, Craig in particular. And now, in the middle of this great adventure, Craig was missing his old friend, too. While he and Matthew got on well, and we were enjoying ourselves as a family, comfortable in each other's company, he was hankering after some company his own age.

Steve had taken Stacey down off her horse, and she was shaky on her legs. As I got down off Lincoln, I realized that the ride had had the same effect on me—and on Cathy too, she admitted. Only Steve—rugged, gentle, experienced Steve—seemed just the same as he'd been when we'd all mounted up back at the ranch.

When Cathy managed to coax Stacey away from Honda—where a deep and meaningful conversation was still taking place, if a little one-sided—we sat down and had our sandwiches and something to drink.

Cathy took photos and was just about to switch on the camcorder when Steve called from the edge of the plateau we were on.

'Come and look here—not too close, mind. The drop here's about three thousand feet.'

I'd never seen anything like it. Dry rocky mountains, deep gorges, glistening necklaces of water, ravines and more space than I'd ever seen in one place before. Suddenly I could feel in me the spirit of Crow Flies High—Harry Sitting Bear's great-grandfather—and his people as they celebrated this exhilarating vastness.

It was weird to reflect that people whose line may have originated in my native Wales have looked upon this unchanged beauty down hundreds of years, and have probably felt the same emotions as were touching me now.

Steve, I noticed, was surprisingly quiet. He hadn't talked much throughout our trek. I'd told him of our reasons for being here, of my wish to talk to the people who had, I believed, descended from my Celtic forebears. We discussed the plight of the Native Americans, and he said he sympathized. But that was as much as he said. Although he was our guide, and guided us well, it was almost as though we were on our own now —now that he'd got us all into the saddle and helped us over our initial apprehensions about the ride ahead.

Perhaps that was how he meant it to be.

Soon we were on our way again. Stacey had been the most eager to get back into the saddle— and resume her conversation with Honda.

We came to a large, clear, open patch of land with a mountainous hill in the distance.

'Right, folks,' Steve announced suddenly. 'Time for a gallop. We'll have to gallop now so the horses can get up some speed to get 'em going up that hill over there.'

'What about Stacey?' Cathy asked —her anxiety of earlier returning anew.

'It's OK,' Steve reassured her. 'Honda'll take good care of her.' Then to Stacey: 'Hold on now—hold on tight.' And with that he galloped off ahead.

'Oh, no, Tony, look!' Cathy said, not without a note of anguish in her voice, as Stacey bounced up and down in the saddle. If it hadn't been for her feet in the stirrups her whole body would have left the horse. 'She's going to come off, she's going to come off!'

The boys, meanwhile, were well away, whooping and yee-ha-ing. Cathy and I tried to hold back our horses, but they had other ideas. They'd seen Honda and the boys' mounts galloping off towards the hill, and they were not going to be left out. So Lincoln and Molly, without much urging from us, raced on ahead until they caught up with the others.

When we reached the top I could feel my heart pounding. Steve told me that once one horse starts to gallop, the others generally follow.

I was surprised how easily we'd all adapted to horse riding—but I had to concede that having well-trained horses was half the battle. Molly—Cathy's dry-land 'canoe' of a horse—was a bit of an exception: she seemed to want to stop when it suited her to munch at the grass. But in our exhilaration and relief at our survival of this escapade, we were able to forgive her.

Chapter Twelve

The lie of the land

Riding through vast expanses of land tends to make my thoughts stray. We just don't see it like this in Wales— beautiful though the landscape in Wales is. We say things like 'unspoilt countryside as far as the eye can see', but in America you can substitute the phrase 'as far as the mind can conceive'.

Ever since man looked at the horizon in one direction, then in another, and realized that between the two horizons was a stretch of earth that he and his tribe or family inhabited, human beings have claimed land and stolen land, have killed and maimed for land, made wars for land, made laws for land. It has happened in North America. It has happened in Wales.

Land of my fathers, land of hope and glory, the promised land, the fatherland, the motherland—all these phrases and more sum up our relationship with the land.

In the Book of Exodus, God is reported as saying he would deliver the Israelites out of the land of the Egyptians and into a land 'flowing with milk and honey'. The land in question was Canaan, to the north. The 'milk and honey' bit is now proverbial for a place of fertility and prosperity.

The phrase 'land of my fathers', well known to me as a Welshman, suggests land that has been 'owned' by generations over millennia. 'Fatherland' and 'motherland' conjure similar sentiments. Yet both of these and 'land of my fathers' also suggest land 'giving birth' to its people. And the phrase 'land of hope and glory'—which forms the title of a song known to every Englishman—sums up the idea of a link between the land and the very qualities of the people living on it.

Every people is associated with a piece of land. Even nomadic tribes would return to a particular territory for hunting or other seasonal reasons. Land is important to us, bound up in our psyche with what it means to be human and have a place in an otherwise impersonal, indifferent world over which we have no control; it's somewhere we can hang our hat and say we belong.

'For each tribe of men God created, he also made a home,' the wild Apache warrior Geronimo is quoted as saying. 'In the land for any particular tribe he placed whatever would be best for the welfare of that tribe.'

Is it any wonder that land is valued on so many levels?

In modern economics, land is bound up in legal terms with ownership and money and title and deeds—rarely thought of as a nurturing mother to all living things. And ever since the proverbial land of milk and honey was promised—and for thousands of years before—man (and it *would* mostly have been the male of the species) has fought over land.

After all, land produces what we need for sustenance. To us, land is little good without our labour—but our labour is not much good without some land on which to perform it. There was an economist in the seventeenth century called Sir William Petty who said, 'While labour is the father and active principle of wealth, earth is the mother.' And 'mother' evokes ideas of something that gives succour and sustenance.

Land also gives us a sense of identity, of who we are—and who we are not. It sets one race apart from another and offers labels with which we are recognized.

At the time of the Norman conquest, all the land belonged to the king, and his principal supporters and nobles were rewarded—with land. For that, they swore allegiance—or fealty—and were asked to perform certain duties, usually military, for the king.

These tenants would repeat the process in effect, parcelling out parts of their land among their own principal supporters.

In modern times, the owner of a piece of land is said to have the freehold, and—subject to planning rules — can do just about what he likes, with no regard to how it might affect people who own or live on neighbouring land.

So bound up are we in the West with ideas of *ownership* of land that we often find it hard to accept that it's not like this everywhere. Not all societies use land as an object of property. Most hunter-gatherer societies—such as most of the American Plains Indians—saw the land much in the way they saw the air they breathed: as something to be shared. (Certain key resources, however, may have been designated, no doubt through negotiation and strife, as subject to certain restrictions and given over into the care of a particular tribe: resources such as water holes in dry areas.)

As we rode through what seemed to us like open land, I reflected that it was not truly 'open' in the sense of being free, yours, mine, anybody's—totally, absolutely unencumbered by laws and obligations. It's subject to many restrictions imposed by humans—some of them for

The Missouri as it meanders through the Badlands.

good reasons, others purely political. We were, after all, riding through a national park—a product of the modern era—yet the dust our horses kicked up was the dust the Plains tribes of centuries ago disturbed to float as glittering motes in the baking sun.

However we look upon land—shared or owned exclusively—there will be someone who will want a slice of it. Or even all of it. We've already seen something of how Wales was fought over. In America, the topography was different, the land bigger, the climate different. But the situation was the same.

It would be overdramatic to say the Welsh had disappeared. Of course we haven't. But our culture is not—cannot be—what it might have been had there not been the incursions of the twelfth and thirteenth centuries, and attempts to subjugate the Welsh since then. It was weakened even further in intervening centuries by political reform.

It was Thomas Cromwell who was responsible for the initial political reorganization. The Act of Union of 1535 united England and Wales, and Wales was assimilated politically to England. Although England's liberties were extended to Wales, so were its laws. While Wales was for the first time given representation in Parliament, the Welsh language was banished from the official proceedings of the courts, and many Welsh customs were abolished.

You'll find that English, too, has long been the official language of America—irrespective of what tribe you belong to. What native languages exist have been kept alive—or struggle to stay alive—by the diligence and nursemaiding of those who care. In Wales we are more fortunate—but controversy continues over our language. In the twentieth century, Welsh is spoken only by a minority, and it has taken the struggles of language activists—some using violent means, but mostly by peaceful process—to allow bilingualism in official circles.

So we can see some parallels—but I'm not claiming, of course, that Wales and the American Indians are the only such parallel. Yet they are *one* parallel, one which happened to be very significant to a Welsh family on the Madoc trail. And the culture of the North American Indian, too, delighted us perhaps more than most, though we were saddened to think that it had been diluted into insignificance, kept alive only in little pockets here and there such as on reservations and places where native ethnicity is valued, studied and respected.

Andrew Jackson, the American President, said in 1832 that the tribes could not exist surrounded by the white settlements and in continual contact with white citizens.

'They have neither the intelligence, the industry, the moral habits, nor the desire of improvement,' he said. 'They must necessarily yield to the force of circumstance and, ere long, disappear.'

White America has ensured that this is almost the case. There were ten million American Indians in the Americas when Columbus landed—and, I assume, a similar number when Madoc landed before him.

There was something else, however, that was totally unforeseen when the white man landed in the New World. What he brought with him would wipe out entire tribes, entire villages, for the natives had no immunity to new diseases brought in by the Europeans, diseases they had not had contact with before. The natives couldn't even take revenge at the microbial level, because they had no epidemic diseases to give back.

The Mandans had already suffered a smallpox epidemic when Lewis and Clark met them at their earth-lodge villages above the Missouri. They would suffer even worse devastation thirty-three years after Lewis and Clark visited them. This we heard about from Luther—although other accounts say it came from contact with other natives who themselves had had contact with white settlements further east.

One account says there were but thirty-nine Mandan survivors of the second epidemic. Another says there were a hundred to a hundred and fifty. Either way, it's a pitifully small number. Other tribes suffered similar fates. We've already seen how badly the three tribes who make up the Fort Berthold reservation were hit by the smallpox epidemics.

But that was not all. The white man wanted land—

Indian land. He might buy it, but quite often he just took it. War and hunger were rife during three centuries as the white tide swept through the Native Americans. There were only about 400,000 Indians in North America by 1840. There were no eastern tribes left—they'd been subdued, annihilated or moved to the west of the Mississippi.

This 'inviolable' Indian country, though, was not immune to greed. The gold rushes to California saw hundreds of covered wagons, loaded with their human cargo and its chattels, invade Indian hunting grounds, devastating grasslands and scaring away the buffalo.

Soon the Indians began to harass the emigrant trains that crossed into the West, or demand tributes for the right of passage through their lands. In September 1851, to prevent what was feared would be a bloody war between the Whites and the Indians, the American government called a very big powwow—a meeting of all the northern tribes—at Horse Creek. Ten Thousand Native Americans gathered, camping in the forests and the valleys in their tepees. Among the gathered Indian nations were the Arikara, the Gros Ventre, Cheyenne, Assinboine and Araphao, as well as the Crow and their sworn enemy, the Sioux.

They were told by Colonel Thomas Fitzpatrick, who addressed them, that the 'Great Father' was aware that 'your buffalo and game are driven off and your grass and timber consumed by the opening of roads the passing of emigrants through your countries.' For those losses, he said, the 'Great Father' wished to make compensation. And so the seeds were sown for the reservation system to begin, as the tribes were offered compensation of $50,000 a year and guns—and told they had to keep away from the trail and keep to designated pieces of land.

There were other treaties signed with other groups of tribes. But they would not succeed, because many natives did not know what they'd signed away. In some cases this amounted to their freedom to roam wherever they chose, and to hunt buffalo. They were told they could not wage war with their bitterest enemies—and in the cases of some tribes this had meant travelling great distances: the Blackfoot of Montana, for example, are known to have travelled as far south as Durango in Mexico to carry out raids.

Native and invader would never live in harmony, it seemed. An incident over a cow led to nearly forty years of war. A young Sioux brave butchered a lame cow, whose white owner had either lost or abandoned it. But the owner demanded $25. A Sioux leader offered two cows. But the owner wanted his $25—nothing else would suffice. The army demanded the surrender of the young warrior—who was called High Forehead—and a young second lieutenant called John L. Grattan, a bit of a boaster who'd claimed he could handle the Indians single-handedly, went into the Sioux camp with thirty-one men. The Indians would not surrender High Forehead and Grattan ordered his men to fire into the village at point-blank range. Grattan and his men were killed when hundreds of Lakota warriors engaged battle.

A year later eighty-six Indians were killed when a brigadier-general was sent by the army to punish the Sioux. A village on Blue Water Creek in Nebraska was destroyed—the first time an entire village had been razed by the white man.

Meanwhile, a young Sioux boy, who had witnessed the massacre, had a vision in which he saw himself as a warrior. When the meaning of the vision was explained to him he was told he would be an undefeated warrior—and his name was changed from Curly to Ta-Sunko-Witko, which is the Sioux name for Crazy Horse. Crazy Horse went on to play an important strategic and military role in the massacre of US forces under General Custer. Having joined Sitting Bull at Little Bighorn, Crazy Horse surrendered in 1877 and was killed some months later while he was in custody in Nebraska.

Although the Native American psyche didn't hold the concept of land ownership in the way we do now, land was firmly behind strife between peoples. It always has been and always will be. Wales was no exception—and nor were the lands of the Native American peoples who now have to live on reservations if they wish to hold on to their ethnicity, their culture, their identity.

Over the years, just as Native America has been inundated by the white man, English settlers had moved to Wales in their droves—all under the protection of English soldiers. At various points in history, the English built towns and got rich at the expense of the Welsh, the Welsh were forced to bring their goods to English markets, were not allowed to carry weapons, could not stay out after nightfall.

I am not trying to say all these things happened at the same time or claim that there's some mystical link between Mandan and Welsh that is regulating their respective destinies. The things I've been reflecting on here happened within different time spans, at different rates. The two lands were very different and the link between the two peoples is really no more dramatic than links that can be traced between many pairs of peoples the world over, if you look hard enough.

But, then, I didn't set out to make fancy claims: only that the link exists, and that a tribe of American Indians in North Dakota is, as you read, struggling to keep alive culture and tradition, in common with many other Indian peoples on their reservations and through their tribal administration offices, while some of its distant cousins in my native Wales strive to keep *their* culture alive. And this 'cousinship' goes much farther back in history than the travels of Christopher Columbus in 1492 and the historic journey on the *Mayflower* by the Pilgrim Fathers in 1620.

Putting aside the questions of conquest and colonization we can see that there are other parallels between the Wales of the time Madoc lived there and the way of life of Madoc's people in America. Many Welsh people lived in solitary huts similar to the Mandans' earth lodges. The Welsh people lived on oats and dairy products provided by their herds. A Welsh person would invite anyone into his home, provided that the visitor first handed over his weapons. Then he—or she—would be given food and drink, and entertained to music and poems. The Mandans show their guests something of the same type of hospitality today as the Welsh have done through the ages.

The Welsh were known, as were the Mandans, for their skill with the spear and the longbow.

There are other parallels, of course, but again we are in danger here of drawing false ones. After all, you can, if you look, find similarities throughout history between one oppressed people and another. However, there are some—such as skills with the blue-glass beads, the type of dwelling, the linguistic similarities—that I believe are significant. Others are of general interest and prove nothing of the link, but serve to bond those twentieth-century Mandan Indians who believe the Madoc legend with like-minded people in my native Wales. One concerns the way the Welsh were treated by the English in many places in history as second-class citizens. So it was with the Native Americans. Good Welsh land was taken from the people—and the Welsh were given land that was inferior: up mountains or too dead to do anything with. Land was seized from the Indians, too. English settlers in Wales had the protection of soldiers. White settlers in North America did, too. The thought that two peoples have spent the last eight centuries developing in different worlds, yet one had branched from the other, is a stimulating and fascinating one.

I began this chapter with some choice phrases that crop up in song and saying, expressing something of humankind's relationship with the land. I'll leave you with another one. It's from 'The Star-Spangled Banner', the national anthem of the United States of America. Just two lines should suffice:

And the star-spangled banner in triumph shall wave
O'er the land of the free and the home of the brave.

And you can interpret the last line as you wish.

Chapter Thirteen

Hand me down that can o' beans

It had begun to get dark. Steve stopped his horse and turned to the rest of us.

'We'll camp here for the night, I guess,' he said. 'We can make an early start in the morning.'

As we wearily unsaddled our horses, Steve lit a fire. Although we were tired, not used riding for long periods as Steve was, I could still feel the excitement in the family that we were about to do what we'd seen a million 'cowboys' do on TV: sit around an open fire at night, under the stars, with the sounds of the prairie around them.

So we sat, with blankets around our shoulders, trying to suck the warmth of the fire into our very bones, as Steve cooked a pile of sausages and a pot of beans.

The kids' eyes lit up at the sight of the sausages. Matthew and Stacey wouldn't even look at a baked bean until they'd devoured the sausage voraciously and demanded more.

Although we *sat* under the stars, we didn't have to sleep under them. There were two tents: one for us and the other for Steve. Although it was cold, we snuggled together for warmth, and it wasn't long before we were all asleep.

'OK, guys, time to get moving!'

I was jolted out of a peaceful sleep as Steve rapped on the tent flap.

Cathy and I got the kids up. We all felt stiff and quite sore. As we emerged yawning and stretching into the crisp Dakota morning, squinting against the light, we saw that Steve had already saddled the horses.

All evidence of our stay here was soon packed away and before we knew it we were making our way to Clyde's. That didn't take us long.

Clyde's wooden cabin was in the middle of nowhere, surrounded by a white picket fence. Steve took our reins and tied the horses to a nearby wooden rail. 'I'll wait here,' he said, and we made our way up the path and were met by a powerfully built Native American aged about seventy. His family were with him in the doorway, including his wife, Inez, and his granddaughters, nineteen-year-old Meranda and five-year-old Malonie.

'Doris said you wouldn't mind if we asked you a few questions,' I said to Clyde as he directed us to various chairs.

'Yes, Doris telephoned me,' he said. 'She said you'd be visiting.'

After introductions to his family and some preliminary chat about our journey—and how the kids would be boasting about their night under the stars once they got back to Wales—I asked Clyde, 'Do you believe there *is* a connection between the Welsh and the Mandans?'

He looked at me for a moment, as if composing his answer. But it was a simple and direct one: 'Yes, I believe it,' he said. 'Because all the stories I've heard, ever since I was a kid—and I'm seventy years old now—well, ever since I was a child I heard stories that the Mandans, since their history began, have had green or blue eyes and light complexions.'

'Have you always lived in the area?' I asked.

'No, we used to live about forty miles down the road.'

'What made you move?'

'Well, it's a long story. See, we moved out of the river bottom to begin with. We were a young married couple then. Well, the government dammed the Missouri River—the Garrison Dam it was called—and flooded us out, so we had to move up to the top.'

Clyde told us about the Garrison Dam, which was started in 1946. Once it was finished, the reservoir covered a massive 155,000 acres of the best farming land on the reservation. The dam had a ruinous effect on the economy of the Fort Berthold Reservation, causing the migration of ninety per cent of the reservation people from their lush and fruitful valley land to high ground.

Before the reservoir was built, the reservation had 600,000 acres of land. So the 155,000 acres taken was equivalent to a little over 25.8 per cent.

The dam also separated the reservation into five sections, which are accessible to each other only by driving many miles around. The government supplied no extra land to replace what had been taken, and people were expected to move to higher ground within the boundaries of the reservation, or move off the reservation altogether and find employment elsewhere.

Most of the children went to schools at a place on the reservation called Elbowoods, but this, too, was inundated by the Garrison Dam. All the children of school age had to change schools when their families were relocated to higher ground. New roads had to be built—about 230 miles of them—because the reservoir covered 80 per cent of the existing roads. The new highway was completed in 1954.

Before the dam altered the lives of the Native Americans of Fort Berthold so dramatically, they lived naturally, using springs and creeks for their water supply. They had plenty of wood and exposed coal for fuel, and plenty of timber for all their building needs. Food was plentiful, with wild fruit and animals in abundance.

When they had to move to higher ground, the nature of their economy changed. Water would have to come from wells. Wells cost money. Fuel would have to be bought. Fuel cost money. The good land was underwater. Now they had to rely far more heavily on money.

'They claim it was for electricity and to irrigate land,' said Clyde bitterly. 'But they only picked on Indian reservations for these dams. It had the effect of joining the three tribes: they mixed us all up and our way of living was changed.'

(Incidentally, before the area was totally inundated, the Smithsonian Institute conducted archaeological research, and uncovered the original Fort Berthold, which was burnt down by the Sioux in 1862.)

'We've been talking to Sitting Bear,' I said. 'He was telling us his father lost good land because of the dam. He was upset because it was his father's land, and he lost it. He told us white settlers came. He said he had to move out of his home, too, and now has to live among others with less room to spread out.'

'Yes,' said Clyde knowingly. 'This housing they have today—you may have to live with neighbours you don't really care for.'

'You're lucky,' I ventured. 'We were talking to a lady the other day—Bernice Mandan. She lives in a unit. It's quite sad.'

'Well,' he sighed, 'we bought this place. We used to live in town but we didn't like it, so we bought this land. It was better when we lived at the river bottom, before the dam. We lived pretty much with nature then. There was timber, berries and animals. We were very self-sufficient then.

'It was good land down there, but not so good up here. We do have a crop up here and some cattle, but it's nothing compared with what we had when I was younger. When we lived down there I never heard the word "welfare". We were independent. We lived altogether different.'

'Are the children losing their old ways?' Cathy asked him.

'Oh, pretty much so,' he said. 'But we're trying to hang on to it, though. The last two generations have been trying to get it back.'

I thought of the Welsh language campaigners back home. I asked Clyde if the children respected the old ways and wanted to see them return.

'Yes, they want to know where they come from,' he said. 'When I was young, younger than my granddaughter there'—he pointed to Meranda, who was sitting opposite me—'it wasn't good to be an Indian. We were taught not to speak our native language.'

Where had I heard *that* before ...?

'I've heard that not many Mandans speak the original language. Is that right?' I asked.

'That's true, sadly,' said Clyde. 'But we're trying to teach the younger people, so we don't lose it altogether.

I showed Clyde my list of words and asked him to compare the Mandan and the Welsh. He agreed that some words were very similar—*too* similar for mere coincidence.

'I do think the Mandans did originate from the Welsh,' he said.

'What about stories?' I asked. 'Are there any stories told about Madoc?'

'There is one,' said Clyde, rubbing his chin thoughtfully. 'One about the Lone Man. He came here from a land far away. He taught the Mandans about planting and building. There are shrines dedicated to him.'

'And you think this Lone Man was Madoc?'

'I think so,' he said. 'It's very probable.'

During the time we spent with Clyde, we talked of the stories he'd heard as a boy. They were usually about people from a faraway land who came to America and eventually mixed with the natives, thus bringing about the Mandan tribe and its strange language and new skills.

Then Meranda piped up. She'd remained fairly quiet during our conversation, listening carefully and intelligently to my questions and her grandfather's answers. She told us she was proud of her heritage, and talked of what she wanted for her people, and of the traditions that she and others like her strove to keep alive.

Meranda was a dancer. When the tribe celebrated their powwow she would dance the Mandan dances, which are as varied as the bright costumes they wear for the occasion.

'Excuse me a moment,' she said, and disappeared from the room, only to arrive back a few moments later with one of the dresses she uses for her dancing. It was called a jingle dress, and was covered with hundreds of small metal cones that jingle together with the slightest movement. It was very heavy—I wondered how she managed to walk in it, let alone dance!

While Cathy and I were talking to Clyde, Inez and Meranda about their native lifestyle, our children were busy entertaining Malonie, who was obviously fascinated by these visitors with their funny accent who had come to talk to Grandpa. She was inquisitive, constantly asking questions about the books that Craig was reading to her. Stacey was patently quite taken by this other little girl, who was bustling about them.

We were interrupted then by Steve, whom we'd left looking after the horses. He said it would soon be time to go if we were to make it back by nightfall. The conversation with Clyde, Inez and Meranda had been fascinating, and time had flown by. We'd almost forgotten about poor Steve. We thanked Clyde and his family, and were soon back in the saddle—all feeling a bit sore, still, from our mammoth riding stint of the day before.

The Williams family meets up wth Clyde's.

Chapter Fourteen

Have a nice day . . .

When we got back to the ranch, the kids were clearly disappointed. They'd loved their horse riding and would dearly love to have done the whole thing again. Cathy and I, from being quite concerned about them when we all first got into the saddle—and even more so when we had to jump a ravine—could see that they would make great riders. Kids are less conscious of safety—especially those of Stacey's age. And they learn better when they're young. And it was Stacey who was the saddest, at having to leave Honda. She wanted us to take him home with us. But in the end I convinced her that this was the best place for him, with other horses in the open space.

Our stay in Indian country was coming to a close. We decided to pay Doris another visit. It was a sad and emotional time for us. Even though we'd met her but once, that meeting had been important to us, as had our meetings with all the folk we were introduced to: Luther Grinnell, Ed Lone Fight, Harry Sitting Bear, Clyde and his family.

Under protest, Doris agreed to have her photo taken. 'Don't tell anyone,' she said conspiratorially. 'My family have been after an up-to-date one of me for years, and I hate having my photograph taken. So keep this to yourselves, OK?'

She told us she planned to visit her father's homeland of Ireland during the summer of 1996. She said that, after making some enquiries there, she believed the Emerald Isle might still be home to some relatives. She was thrilled at the prospect of finding her father's kin.

And so we said our cheerios, and soon we were all silently looking up at a large square sign that said, quite without emotion: YOU ARE NOW LEAVING THE FORT BERTHOLD RESERVATION. You almost expected it to add, 'So take care, and have a nice day . . .'

Within the past few months we had entered two worlds that were very different from ours, both with a sense of peace, tranquillity, stillness of spirit. One was an uninhabited island in the South Seas. Another was a land that some of my forefathers—countrymen if not actual ancestors—helped to people.

We spoke much during our flight back to Britain about the friendships we'd made in such a short space of time. We decided that perhaps we'd never truly settle, that we as a family loved to wonder and to explore. Soon the children will be old enough make up their own minds about what areas of the globe they wish to see. And Cathy and I hope they do. They say travel broadens the mind. It's an old cliché, but, like a lot of old clichés, it's true.

Who knows where Cathy and I will end up? She hankers for North Dakota; I hanker for the South Seas. We can't live in *both* places and stay together. Maybe one day we'll find somewhere that suits us both.

But we were on our way home—and our wonderful relationship with the Mandans wasn't over yet. The more we looked at the similarities between some Welsh customs and artefacts and those of the Mandans, the more convinced I was that these were more than mere coincidence: the earth lodges, the bull boats that are so similar to the Welsh coracles, the blue beads, the language connection, the beliefs of the Mandans themselves.

Lewis and Clark, Verendrye and even Raleigh met so many Native Americans, but singled out the Mandans as being different from other tribes they had met—and similar to the early Celts. I suppose people will continue to deny that Madoc ever existed in America, but I have visited the people of the Fort Berthold reservation, and that has been enough to convince me otherwise.

Soon, although we didn't know it yet, we'd be looking forward to a return trip to North Dakota, specifically to observe for ourselves the Mandan powwow—and to get a steamy taste of the famous sweat lodge.

And we had a television programme to take part in. We would be back . . .

Arrivals are always better than departures!

Part Two:

Our TV times

Chapter Fifteen

Letter to Auntie

May 1996. We are once again in Minneapolis. It is six months since our last visit. This time, Cathy is my sole companion, the kids having been left at home with Cathy's mother, Brenda.

We are soon to meet Alan Ereira, a film producer and director, at Minot. This has come about because I sent a draft of a proposed book on the Madoc-Mandan link—the draft that eventually became this book—to a friend in London. That friend sent it to Alan. He was intrigued with the story, and within days was at our house in Swansea to discuss a proposed documentary.

In fact, he said it had come at just the right time, because he'd recently retired from the BBC after thirty years and was about to launch an independent company called Sunstone Films. He wanted to do a documentary—scheduled for transmission in early 1997—about the theory that other people visited America before Columbus set foot there.

My conviction and research would be at the heart of the programme, he said.

This was in February 1996. I gave Alan the information he needed to write to the Beeb with a proposal. He suggested two trips to North America—one for the recce and the other for filming. Within a few weeks, the BBC had agreed on a contract for the programme, and the preparations for our journey were under way.

The first trip would involve Alan, Cathy and me. We were to introduce him to the Mandan people we had met, and he would decide on what location shots he would need and who would be best for interviewing.

So here we were, Cathy and I, in Minneapolis, and who should we meet but the immigration woman who'd seemed so contemptuous of our research when we were here last time.

And she remembered us!

'Ah,' she said. 'You guys are back. For how long this time?' She inspected our passports.

'Just ten days,' I told her.

She didn't bombard us with questions this time, not after noticing that we'd been granted visas by the US Embassy in London. So we got through with minimum fuss.

'I hope it's that easy when we return with the kids to do the filming,' said Cathy as we walked away.

We met Alan in Minot the following day. He was a bit weary after driving four hundred miles. He walked into the bar of the Ramada Hotel, where we had stayed the night. He was an imposing sight: all six foot of him, with his beard and stetson. He wore brown sandals and was surrounded by his own cigar smoke.

Alan's something of a historian, and has made many wonderful documentaries. He's also written several books, one being *The Elder Brothers*, which is about the Kogi people of the Sierra Nevada range in California, and his experiences of living with them.

'Ah, there you are,' he said as he spotted us at the bar. Eyeing our drinks, he added. 'Just what I need.' He ordered a margarita.

'How was your drive down?' I asked.

'Long. But at least the roads were clear.'

We had planned to eat at the Ramada, but Alan suggested going straight to the reservation. We could eat there.

As we entered the reservation I felt a sort of spiritual warmth—especially when I looked behind me at that sign again that said YOU ARE NOW LEAVING THE FORT BERTHOLD RESERVATION. Not yet, I wasn't.

Suddenly I felt relaxed again. Alan laughed when I said I felt as though I were no longer in the United States of America, but somewhere altogether different.

We were booked into the Four Bears Lodge, which is close to the Four Bears Bridge. The lodge is part of the casino. It doesn't exactly enhance its surroundings, but it serves a purpose on the reservation—and plays its part in keeping unemployment down.

The travelling had caught up with us and, after tucking into a meal of steak—steak the way the Americans like it—and all the trimmings, we decided it was time to hit the sack.

Cathy and I slept like logs.

We had an 8.30 meeting in the reservation office with Ed Lone Fight, who was there right on time. I made the necessary introductions, and we discussed plans for the documentary.

'I think it's a good idea,' Ed told us as he made notes of our plans in a small book.

'Good,' Alan said brightly. 'I'm so pleased.'

'I think we should go to Mandaree,' Ed said, rising from his seat. 'I've got some people I want you to meet.'

Mandaree, in another part of the reservation, was a

forty-minute drive from where we were in New Town. I decided to travel with Ed; Cathy and Alan followed in the car Alan had hired. On our journey towards Mandaree, Ed slowed the car.

'Tony, we will have to be silent for a while so that I can show my respect for the sacred bundle,' he said. He prayed for a while, then threw some tobacco out of the car window. I decided not to ask the significance of all of this. Not just yet, anyhow.

We had our meeting in what Ed called 'the office'. It was a large room with a long table with chairs on two sides at one end, and another, smaller, table at the other end, which held a flask of coffee and some cups.

We were here to meet, for the first time, Louella Youngbear, an elderly Native American, part Mandan. Her daughter, Kathy, who was to become Alan's assistant during our stay was also there, and we also met two elderly Native men, Ned and William, and a very European-looking woman called Eunice—but she was Native American. Her Indian name— in English, anyway—was Sweetgrass.

As the meeting was about to begin, Luther Grinnell made a late entrance. He recognized us instantly, and his first question was, 'Where are your children?'

'They'll be coming over with us when we come back in a week or so,' Cathy told him as he sat down next to her.

We all turned our attention to Alan, who began explaining what type of filming he was aiming to do, and what he hoped the outcome would be. He would want interviews, he said, and would want to film some of the forthcoming powwow festival. He'd need establishing shots, of course, of the beautiful countryside and parts of the reservation.

I wondered what they were thinking, these people, as this energetic Englishman explained in his very English accent that he wanted to make a film about a seafaring prince who may have been ancestor to both them and the Welsh thousands of miles away.

It had been a successful and enjoyable meeting. We returned to the hotel at Four Bears, where we were to meet Doris McGrady for dinner. She seemed as pleased to see us as we were to see her—although I got the impression she didn't take too well to Alan. She seemed a little aloof with him, and I think he sensed this.

It wasn't an entirely comfortable meeting because of this, but we did learn more about Doris and her people, and she told us over dinner that she was going to take a year off from her job to study more and fulfil a promise to herself that she would do more travelling. The conversation soon steered its way around to Madoc.

'There aren't many Mandans who know the legend,' she said. 'I could count them on my two hands.'

'So what makes *you* believe?' Alan asked.

'Five reasons,' Doris replied, as though she'd enumerated them before and was practised in imparting this particular information. 'One, the boats. We were the only tribe to use the bull boats, which are very similar to the Welsh coracle.

'Two, the structure of the Celtic houses of old—very much the same as the earth lodge.

'Three, the similarity with certain words.

'Four, the Lone Man story, which may have only come about after the arrival of Madoc.

'Five, the skill of making the blue-glass beads, which are only made by the Mandans, but also, I believe, were made in some parts of Wales.'

Alan questioned her further on her beliefs, and she had an answer for all his queries. As she was about to leave, she told Cathy that she would like to see us again—on our own. She didn't like Alan.

Well, Alan had been invited by Ed Lone Fight to see a sweat lodge the following day, so we used the time to visit Doris at her home. We talked at length about Madoc, and about Doris's planned journey to Ireland—and possibly Wales.

She seemed far more at ease than she had been the previous day.

On our return to Four Bears, we discovered that Alan still hadn't returned, so we spent some time walking along the banks of the Missouri.

Early the next morning, while we were having breakfast, we were joined by a friend of Alan's whom he'd met on a previous project. She was Joanna, and she had with her a friend and colleague, Maggie, a Native American from the Hopi people. Both had been involved in keeping alive the language of the Hopi tribe, and were here to see if she could do a similar job with the Mandans.

I was reminded of Wales, where classes in our language are held in colleges and community centres throughout the country, attended by native (but non-Welsh-speaking) Welsh people and English incomers alike.

Today we were to visit Edwin Benson at Twin Buttes, with a stopover along the way at Little Knife River. I wanted to show Alan the earth lodge and a bull boat.

With Joanna, Maggie and Kathy Youngbear, there was quite a group of us. Kathy, Cathy and I travelled in one car, while Joanna, Alan and Maggie were in the other.

At Little Knife River, something strange happened. With the memory of Ed Lone Fight's plug of tobacco still vivid in my mind, I now witnessed another act that exemplified the culture of those who seek to preserve what once was. Kathy Youngbear suddenly became quite emotional. She left the path we were walking along and stepped on to the sacred ground where the earth lodges had once stood. This was the last natural settlement of the Mandans, before the smallpox epidemic took hold and caused so much suffering and loss. Fifty or more indents on the ground marked where the lodges of Awatixa village had once stood. Kathy let down her hair and fell to her knees, crying and praying in her native tongue.

Cathy and I could only look on, not quite knowing what to say—or if we should say anything at all. I suppose

The village at Knife River, where indents mark the site of the earth-lodges of old.

it's part of the notorious British reserve, but you can't help but feel like an intruder at times like this. And yet it's odd, because the act Kathy Youngbear was performing at this moment was one that had been performed in public by generations of Native Americans of all tribes: the naked, unashamed demonstration of one's religious faith in all its fiery fervour and unimpeded passion.

Alan seemed to take it all in his stride, man of the world that he was.

When Kathy returned from the piece of sacred ground, she said we had to make an offering. Alan knew immediately what to do. He reached into his jacket pocket and brought out a pouch of his ever-dwindling tobacco. Kathy took some, threw it on to the ground, and then left us again and walked once more on to the ground on which she had made obeisance in such a dramatic manner. Later she told us she had prayed to the spirits for permission to be there, where so much tragedy had taken place.

Maggie began to share whatever spiritual passions Kathy Youngbear had just expressed, and went over to a small hillock, where she knelt. The rest of us stood in silence.

When the two women had finished praying, they returned to us. 'We have to leave this place now,' said Kathy, who had tears running down her face. 'And don't forget to call your spirits back to you before you get back into your cars.'

On reaching the cars, Cathy asked, 'Why do we have to call our spirits back?'

'If you don't,' Kathy explained, 'they will be left here in limbo.' We did as we were told.

Edwin Benson—who was Kathy Youngbear's uncle—lived in a cabin-style house surrounded by endless prairie. He greeted us warmly and we were pleasantly surprised to see that an abundant feast had been prepared by his wife Eunice in our honour: home-grown corn on the cob, potatoes, home-made beef and vegetable soup, slices of cooked beef that was so tender that it fell apart as it was picked up. And to top it all, a large slice of home-made apple pie. What else?

After our repast we settled down and spoke to Edwin and Eunice about Alan's plans for a documentary. Edwin told us about old customs, many of them no longer practised. One was the Sun Dance, a ritual in which, years ago, the male natives would puncture their skin. Some would even be hung up by their skin, which would be pierced.

I was reminded of that Richard Harris film, *A Man Called Horse*, in which the very same ceremony—subsequently made illegal by the US government—was performed on the hero, played by Harris. It was intended to prove his manhood by displaying his ability to withstand pain. The Harris character, nicknamed Horse, was living among the natives and almost became one of them. But he had to prove himself. During the ceremony, sharp claws—possibly bears'—were attached to ropes, and then pushed into the skin of his pectorals and secured. As if that was not painful enough, he would then be hauled aloft into the roof of the lodge, way up above the central fire.

The magicians of the film world had encased Harris in a false torso of some kind, giving him a new 'skin'. Either that or the poor chap's walking round with two very nasty scars on his chest . . .

'Many years ago,' said Edwin, 'when the Sun Dance was performed, a person would chop off one of his arms, and, because the ceremony is very spiritual, the others taking part could pick up the severed arm and attach it back on to the injured man. It would be the same as it was before he had cut it off.

'Now one year, a man thought he could do better, so he had his head chopped off. But, when the others tried to put the head back on, it wouldn't go, and of course the man was dead. Since then they decided to change the ceremony, and now they call it *okapi*, which means "only part".'

Cathy and I looked at each other. Was Edwin joking? Trying to give us a scare?

But Edwin was very knowledgeable about custom and was a highly respected member of the reservation, so maybe there was some truth in the stories. Edwin was one of the few who had sacred bundles, passed down from father to son within families, and used in religious ceremonies. If the male line was broken, the bundle would be buried with its last custodian.

Edwin's bundle was made of turtle shells and various secret clan items. I was reminded of the bundle Luther had told us about during our first visit.

Edwin was also the keeper of the Lone Man shrine. Clyde Baker had told us about such shrines and Edwin took us out now to the quite remote ground where the shrine is situated. We drove some way but the last half a mile had to be on foot, and it was quite a climb. The shrine was a circle of wooden posts, about four foot high. Wrapped around the posts was a band of red cloth intended to mark the level of flood-water, for the Lone Man is a Noah-figure.

Stories about him abound, and central to them all is the idea of collecting people and animals on a boat, and the survival of this boat in a flood. I began to wonder if the Lone Man and Madoc were one and the same. You might argue that the Mandans were told this story by others who know the legend of Noah's ark from the Bible. It's also true that similar-sounding stories (virgin births, resurrection and other phenomena) occur in many religious myths and legends, and the Noah or Lone Man tale was just one of them. But what makes it odd is that the Lone Man seems to be strictly a Mandan tale, not told by other Native American tribes.

After a fruitful talk with Edwin and Eunice, we left Twin Buttes. I felt that perhaps today I'd moved closer to the shadow of Madoc. The Lone Man was particularly interesting and, who knows, the arrival of Madoc and his ships could well have been the inspiration for the legend.

Our start the following day was slower. Alan had got an infection in his thumb and it was badly swollen. He needed medical attention, but, it being a Sunday, the only place he could get treated was a hospital in Watford City. Fortunately, it was only an hour's drive away from the reservation.

It seemed pointless that we should all go, so Joanna and Maggie accompanied Alan, and Cathy and I arranged to meet them at Twin Buttes. We collected Kathy Youngbear from her home—an attractive, three-bedroomed unit that overlooked the town of Mandaree. We then continued our journey to Twin Buttes, driving through some spectacular landscapes. We even spotted some white-tailed deer here and there.

When we met up with Alan, he was in some pain. The doctor had lanced his thumb without an anaesthetic, and Alan was none too pleased. We were quite glad to let him explore Twin Buttes by himself—in pursuit of people who might eventually be involved in the film—and Cathy and I had some time on our own at last.

When Alan returned, he was very excited. It had been a very promising day, he said, and we'd be doing most of the filming at Twin Buttes. Preparations were afoot for the forthcoming pow-wow there, and it seemed that when we returned to film, a great number of key people would be at Twin Buttes for the celebrations. The pow-wow is an annual celebration of the Mandans' culture—a festival of music, dance, ritual and ceremonies.

We'd been to see the pow-wow ground with Kathy Youngbear and her mother Louella.

The site for the pow-wow just outside Twin Buttes was, as you might imagine, on sacred land. A circular shelter had been erected made up of three sections with entrances between them. For the night-time celebrations, there were huge lights set on poles surrounding the site. A great many people were involved in clearing the site, preparing huts as souvenir stalls and so on. While we were looking round we were interested to hear from Louella that there were more speakers of the Mandan tongue than we'd at first realized, and the language was being taught to schoolkids by a woman called Lydia Sage, who also taught adult classes.

Well, we would be back this year for the great celebration and might hear for ourselves how much Mandan is spoken at a time when friends and families get together to enjoy themselves. But we had a trip home to make before that.

On our last day of this reconnaissance trip we said our goodbyes to Joanna and Maggie and then Alan, Cathy and I travelled south to Bismarck, the capital city of North Dakota, to see what information the museum there had on the Mandans. On our arrival, we met a historian called Richard, who showed us first what was on public display, and then gave us passes to see the archives.

As he showed us down, we stopped by an office and looked at some photographs. Then we met an archaeologist who did his utmost to pour cold water on our research. He told us the Mandans had no connection with the Welsh at all; he knew all there was to know about the tribe, he said.

'What about the stories told by the Mandans of the blue-eyed, blond Indians?' Alan asked.

'A myth,' said our archaeologist, whose name we didn't get. 'Created by the white men and passed on to the Indians.' He believed that Europeans were the only races that could retrace their histories, because they wrote everything down. The Celts and American Indians, on the other hand, related their history by word of mouth. This seemed to convince him that there could never be any worthwhile evidence for a link.

Yet much has been passed on by word of mouth before it got into print—including much in the Bible. I wasn't inclined to take his word, and nor were Cathy and Alan. I'm happy to have an open mind about things, but academics can sometimes show an arrogance borne out of fear of losing the big badge they wear that says in bright shiny letters: I AM AN EXPERT, FOLKS.

155

Richard interrupted the conversation with the archaeologist. 'I have something that might interest you,' he said. So we followed him into a storeroom filled with antiques: stuffed animals, costumes of various tribes —all very well preserved—Indian jewellery, headdresses, moccasins. They were all packed in drawers and labelled. Then we were shown a scroll, about twenty-five feet long, nine inches wide. It had been made by a Mandan called White Rabbit in 1910. He was the last of what the Indians called 'scattercorn priests'. They are key figures in fertility rituals—ceremonies at times of planting and harvesting, intended to secure good harvests. We'd been shown pictures of White Rabbit at Edwin Benson's home, and one hung in Edwin's living room.

The scroll was a fascinating piece of Indian history, which gave the lie to our archaeologist friend's claim that only word of mouth was used to pass on historical facts through the generations. It depicted White Rabbit's ancestors through thirty-three generations—all scattercorn priests. All their names were there with their colourful likenesses. White Rabbit had been the one who completed the scroll, as he had no sons to carry on the tradition. So he took the secrets of the scattercorn priests to the grave with him. Interestingly, Lydia Sage, who teaches the Mandan language to old and young, is White Rabbit's grand-daughter.

The scroll he made—covering generations—is proof that matters important to the Indians *were* recorded, kept safely, and handed down. The written word is not the only way to preserve history. Yes, minor detail might get skewed a little in the telling, but major facts are likely to be preserved, because it is important to the people whose history it is to keep that history faithfully for the benefit of future generations.

It had been an instructive day. The more I chatted to Mandans and other Native Americans, the more I saw of their culture, the more convinced I became of their succession from our Prince Madoc.

Chapter Sixteen

Camera, action . . .

June 1996. We are in Minot again. This time the children are with us.

We'd booked once more to stay in the Ramada Hotel. It had taken us twenty-two hours to get here and we were all thoroughly exhausted.

No sooner had I settled down to sleep, it seemed, than it was time to get up. We all went down for breakfast, and afterwards Cathy and I went over to the airport to pick up a car Alan had hired for our use. We loaded luggage and children into the car and drove to Bismarck, where we were to meet the rest of the crew. We booked into the Radison Hotel. The crew was not expected until later in the evening, so Cathy and I enjoyed our free time swimming with the children and playing arcade games.

We met up with the film crew at breakfast the following morning: Alan, his personal assistant Jill Dales, the sound man Mike Savage, the cameraman Bill Broomfield and his assistant Hugh Adams.

We were excited. Who wouldn't be? We'd had no experience of making a film before, and, while these guys sat around nonchalantly talking of the day's shoot, Cathy and I had to suppress our enthusiasm a bit—adopt an attitude of 'been there, done that, bought the T-shirt'—in case we were thought naive and childish.

Soon we were on our way. Cathy and I were filmed leaving the Radison Hotel. It's all so seamless by the time a film reaches the screen, but the amount of preparation that goes into such a simple shot is surprising if you've never been involved before.

Alan would order an establishing shot. This puts what's to come into some sort of perspective. Even such a seemingly simple shot is agonized over, as director and cinematographer discuss angles and lighting. As we would learn throughout the filming procedure, many things would be shot twice. What you eventually see on the screen of, say, someone being interviewed and then the interviewer's face nodding is actually shot in two takes—unless you have the luxury of two cameras. Some film-makers call it 'doing the noddies'. It was odd to think that the nodding news interviewers on *News at Ten* and *Wales Today* are just nodding either at a silent interviewee who's had the procedure explained to him, or are nodding into thin air. I wondered why it often looked so false. Now I know.

Anyway, here we were, walking out of the Radison Hotel into the morning sunlight, trying not to think of the camera watching us with its electronic eye and three or four people standing behind it observing our progress.

Then we were on our way to Little Knife River village, where Cathy and I were to be filmed interviewing Harry Sitting Bear.

We didn't know we passed through a time zone and were an hour earlier than we thought. The village ranger was helpful, giving the children a quiz on the Mandans and Hidatsa, on local flora and fauna, native lifestyles. The kids did well. They'd learned a lot already. When they scored high marks, they were issued with ranger badges and certificates.

At Little Knife River, apprehensively waiting for Harry, our interviewee.

When Harry arrived, Cathy and I interviewed him in an earth lodge. Harry was sensitive to our apprehension. If walking out of a hotel into the sunlight had bothered us, what would conducting an interview be like?

'Don't worry,' said Harry, putting an arm on my shoulder. 'We both feel apprehensive. But we'll see the interview through together.'

I was anxious about something else, though, not just the actual filming and trying not to dry up. I had, through my nosing about in Mandan affairs, brought about this documentary. I wanted it to go well for the Mandans. I was aware, as was Harry, that we were now at the mercy of the film-makers. Harry sensed this anxiety, I'm sure.

'There's a purpose to everything,' he said. 'You coming over here, searching. I believe everything will be good. This programme will be a voice for us all.'

'I hope—' I cleared my throat and tried again. 'I hope so.'

The interview went well. Mike, the sound man, remarked afterwards how quiet it was—no fidgeting, throat-clearing, breathing too heavily when not talking, that kind of thing.

I put that down to Harry's natural serenity. I also do quite a lot of meditation, and attention to breathing, as anyone who's ever done it will know, is a vital part of the process. I suppose I've learned to sit calmly over the years and it had come in handy now.

Harry told us—and the camera—about his people, and his thoughts on the link with Prince Madoc, of pride of his ancestors and of the history of the tribes who inhabit the Fort Berthold reservation.

We were booked into a motel in the small town of Halliday, just off the reservation, for the rest of the filming. On our way back there we became part of a scene I've only ever seen in movies. We'd decided on a leisurely journey back, so took one or two detours along country lanes. The kids were in the back of the car, music emanated from the radio, Cathy sang along. The scenery was a joy to behold.

Then I looked into my rear-view mirror and saw the blue and red lights of a patrol car —gaining on us fast. I thought I'd better pull over.

Out stepped a burly cop, leather-garbed and sporting the seemingly compulsory dark glasses. He sauntered towards us, gun holstered to his waist.

'I think he's going to lock us up in one of his cells,' said Matthew, his voice lowered in a mixture of fear and excitement.

'Shush, Math,' Craig hissed.

The officer was now standing by the car door. His voice was dark-brown and rich, as though he were an actor who'd played this part in a movie and decided he'd like to do it as a job.

'Step out of the car, please, and follow me.'

With a badly hidden gulp, I did as I was told, hoping that my Welsh accent and a few smiles would save the day. He walked to his car and sat inside, motioning for me to look in.

'See that?' He pointed to some sort of display on a screen. 'That's a speed monitor. You were speeding.'

'I was only doing thirty-three,' I protested weakly—and politely.

'The speed limit here is twenty-five,' he said. 'You were doing eight miles per hour over the limit.'

All I could think to do was apologize.

'Where you guys heading?' he asked.

'We're on our way to Halliday. We're staying there.'

'Are you with the English people we passed earlier?' That must have been Alan and the crew. They were ahead of us.

'Er, yes.'

'Hmm. Well *they* were speeding, too. *Twenty* miles an hour over the limit.'

For some reason this made me feel a little easier. My crime was only forty per cent as heinous.

'So what happens now?' I dreaded the answer.

'I'm going to have to fine you,' he said, and handed me a slip of paper. 'Pay within twenty-one days. The address is there.'

I returned to the car heaving a sigh of relief. Four faces gawped at me, wondering what was going to happen. I showed them the slip, and we all burst out laughing.

The next day I stopped off at a post office and paid the fine. It amused me to see that the town near which I had been caught out was Dodge!

Chapter Seventeen

Thunder and lightning,
very very frightening ...

It was the evening of the powwow. We could hear the drums, echoing hauntingly all around us. We'd arranged to meet Louella there for a filmed interview. We were getting used to it now—feeling like old hands. Almost. After my first attempts, all I could say was thanks for the cutting-room floor. I'm sure many of my ahems, ums, ahs and long pauses would end up there. I was trusting Alan and his editor to transform me from a gibbering idiot into a seasoned interviewer, all with the magic of the editing machine.

As we approached the site we could see dozens of tents that had been erected there for the festivities. But it didn't look like a good night for a party—or an interview. The sky was frowning blackly, and then came the lightning.

We found Louella, and she and Alan decided we'd best do the interview just off the powwow site, somewhere more open where the light was better. So we all trooped off to what turned out to be an ideal spot, giving us a backdrop of spectacular open countryside, with the silver ribbon of a vast river in the distance.

'I should have put on my Indian costume,' said Louella, as Mike checked the sound, and Alan, Bill and Hugh got us into position and did mysterious things with light meters. 'If you come back on Monday, I'll wear it for you.'

But we had a schedule, and the interview had to go ahead as she was.

After some preliminary chat, we asked her about a particular story she'd mentioned to us as being part of her folk history—a story of a magic boat.

'A long time ago, there was a boat that took our people from place to place,' she said. 'It was not like any other boat. It was a magic boat that would move by the command of your voice. At the head of the boat there was a carved animal head.

'The people would tell the boat to take them across the river, and the boat would take them. Then it would fetch the others back who wanted to come back to the village.

'Now there was a young foolish man who did not believe what the others told him about the boat, so he decided to test it for himself. He told the boat to go away, and the boat went. And it has never come back. Because no one told it to.'

It was a lesson in faith, we supposed, and in respecting the stories of your ancestors without question.

She told us more about her people, and then Alan signalled for us to wind up. Louella hugged the children as we were packing. 'I wish these were my grandchildren,' she said.

We thanked Louella for her story and her interview.

'You're very welcome,' she said. 'I know you and Cathy are here to search for the link between our peoples. If there is anything else I can do for you in the future I will.'

'Thanks, Louella,' Cathy and I said in unison.

It was fortunate that we'd filmed when we did. As soon as we got back to the powwow ground, the skies opened. Lightning lacerated the sky and thunder cracked and rumbled. The rain was merciless, stinging in its fury. The celebrations were postponed until the following day.

Disappointed, we drove back towards our hotel. The children seemed to think it would be safer there, anyway. They hadn't seen anything quite like this. A mixture of excitement and fear gripped them as they watched the storm through the car windows, saw lightning hitting the ground quite close by. They must have thought a brawl had broken out at a gods' disco.

I was reminded of Cathy's mother, Brenda. She hates storms.

'Good job she's not here,' I said.

At the first hint of lightning, Brenda would retreat to the safety of the darkest corner she could find. But there was no protection for us, stuck in our hired car with thunder, lightning and rain battling for supremacy all around us.

Then Stacey screamed.

'My God!' said Cathy. 'That nearly hit us. Get us back to the hotel. Quick!'

Once within the comparative safety of the hotel, we closed the curtains and decided to have an early night.

The next day was bright and sunny. It was as though there had never been a storm the night before. We had breakfast in the town, remarking on how it reminded us of something from a fifties road movie. There was a bank, a supermarket, a post office, the café we were eating in, a couple of bars. And that was about it. Far from finding it tatty, we thought it thoroughly charming and evocative.

Our next interview was to be with Edwin Benson. So we all went off to the pow-wow site to pick him up. He took us back to the Lone Man Shrine—way out in the wilderness.

Edwin made an offering of tobacco—pushing it in to the circle inside the wooden posts—and said a prayer in his native tongue.

During the interview, Edwin told us again about the Lone Man legend, how he had come from far away and taught the Mandans about building and planting. We would find out more about the Lone Man in our interview with Ed Lone Fight the following day, but for now we all went back to the pow-wow site—and a feast that awaited us.

Pow-wow participants in native dress: favourite colours were scarlet, bright yellow or orange and vivid blues.

We'd been invited to join the rest of the spectators—including the Governor of North Dakota, Ed Schafer, and his wife Nancy—and the pow-wow participants in a most abundant feast of beef, potatoes, beans, pasta and a host of other things.

The day was enlivened even further by colourful, energetic dancing by young natives in dazzling costumes. All of them were handmade, and some must have taken weeks to create.

Although we were here doing research and helping to make a documentary, we couldn't resist entering into the spirit of things like typical tourists, and taking a lot of photographs for our album.

It was against the background of the Killdeer Mountains that we were to interview Ed Lone Fight, who had donned a suit for the occasion. We crossed some fields until we came to the edge of a cliff overlooking the mountain view. The peaks seemed to go on for ever.

'Did all the land we see around us once belong to the three tribes?' I asked Ed by way of an opener.

'Yes,' he said. 'All this was our land, but due to the dam and the government our lands have been greatly reduced.'

We moved on to the Lone Man legend, and Cathy asked if it was peculiar to the Mandan people.

'Yes, that story is what sets the Mandans apart from other tribes,' he said. 'The Mandans talk of the Lone Man, while other tribes talk of the Creator. There is a difference in the tales. The Lone Man is said to be the creator of cattle—among other things—while the Creator created buffalo. Maybe that is the link you are looking for. The

Lone Man stories are about European cattle, while other tribes talk of buffalo.'

'What do you think of the idea of being connected to the Welsh?' I asked. 'And do the Mandans accept the legend?'

Without evading my question, Ed said there were many things in the Mandans' history that concerned him, and the smallpox epidemics had wiped out many people, and much oral tradition.

'But the connection is always there,' he said. 'We accept it as part of our lives. My grandfather, you know, had a spot of ginger hair on his head.'

It was as if the argument had been clinched once and for all.

The next stars of our documentary were to be the buffalo that had played such a large part in the lives of the Plains Indians for so many centuries. First we had to find them.

We drove past Mandaree to Skunk Creek Bay—a place with the sort of name I thought I'd only ever encounter in a Western movie. The herd belongs to the three tribes and roams hundreds of acres of land at the edge of a lake.

We were helped by Bob, who looked after the herd. He opened a large gate that was chained shut, and we all drove through. After a sharp turn to the left we found ourselves almost hidden by grass. Only tyre tracks enabled us to see where we were going.

As we bumped over humps and screeched across small ditches, the kids thought we were filming for a James Bond film rather than a TV documentary, and we were in hot pursuit of villains.

When we all got out of our vehicles, I turned to Mike, the sound man, and commented, 'No one would treat their own cars like that.'

'Don't worry,' he said. 'They're only hire cars.'

Suddenly Bob shouted, 'There!' We all looked, and saw some of the herd grazing peacefully near a gully. The fact that there were only a few of them brought home to me the way these animals, too, had been reduced to such pitifully small numbers by the march of time and 'progress'. I was reminded of that spectacular scene from *Dances with Wolves*, in which the buffalo in their hundreds, maybe thousands, thundered across the screen. And here were a handful of them, grazing contentedly, looking quite harmless and almost cuddly.

Yet, like the Mandans, they had survived, and also looked proud and noble as they grazed.

Bill, the cameraman, and his assistant Hugh managed to get quite close for a while, filming them as they grazed. Then the great creatures became uneasy and stampeded away down into the valley.

While the crew were packing away their gear, and Cathy and I took photos of the view, Matthew ran up to us full of excitement clutching some object whose origin we could only guess at.

'Look,' he said. 'Look what Bob gave me.' In his hand was a large tooth. 'It's a buffalo tooth,' he said proudly 'And I'm taking it home.'

The next day was to be our last day of filming in the US. We were to interview Kathy Youngbear—and again we would be at the powwow ground. The place was almost deserted now the celebrations were over. A few tents remained, but their owners were taking them down and preparing to go. A few scavenging birds scoured the ground for any titbits that had been dropped during the weekend's festivities.

Kathy Youngbear was wearing her hair in a ponytail, and wore sunglasses to hide eyes swollen by being out in the sun for too long. The weekend in the open, and the Sun Dance, had left their mark.

I was impressed by Kathy's performance during the interview. It was as though she'd done all of this sort of thing before—and maybe she had. Her voice was strong and confident, that of someone who had something to say. And this interview was about to turn into one of the more remarkable of our time filming, because of what Kathy said to us.

First, she spoke of the arrival of Columbus which she saw as the start of the unwelcome European invasion of her native land. At one point, quite surprisingly, she paused and turned to Alan.

'Have you got any of those cigars you smoke to spare?' she asked.

'Yes,' he said, taken aback.

'They smell nice,' said Kathy. 'I'd like to try one.'

'OK,' said Alan. 'I'll let you have a packet after the interview.'

And we resumed. Kathy turned back to the camera and talked of how her ancestors were light-skinned and fair-haired. Then she turned to face Cathy and me, saying, 'I've got to know you two personally, and I believe you people are doing a good thing. I wasn't sure what you expected when I first met you. You were just some white people who wanted something from us. But now I know you are honest, genuine people, and I feel a bond with you.'

Her words made me feel proud. These people, I reflected, had every right to be suspicious of outsiders, after all they'd been through—and were still going through today. To have gained their trust like this was a great honour. I could understand why Cathy loved this part of America and its people: they were kind, likeable, honest people and their warmth was quite overwhelming.

Our day of filming had come to an end. We hugged Kathy Youngbear—although there was one final thing she'd be doing for us. She was to guide Alan and the crew to Edwin Benson's house to get a shot of the picture of White Rabbit, which hung on the wall at his home.

As for Cathy and me, we were on our own. We were to be part of the crew again in Wales, but for now we had a little time to spare—and we'd been invited to take part in a communal sweat.

Chapter Eighteen

Some like it hot

We headed back to Mandaree, where Georgia Fox lived. We'd met her briefly during our first visit with Alan. It seemed months before, yet it was little more than two weeks. She'd made her invitation then, but we decided we'd wait until this visit so the children could take part, too.

Craig was a little apprehensive. 'What if we see spirits?' he asked.

Matthew, on the other hand, *wanted* to see something supernatural if the opportunity presented itself.

We pulled up outside Georgia's trailer home. She must have heard us, because she came out to greet us. Georgia and her sister Nina live in the trailer with Georgia's little daughter Sky. Georgia was in her late thirties, and sported long black hair, which she wore tied back.

Sky couldn't wait to get Stacey inside, to have another little girl to play with. 'Do you want to come play with me?' she asked. Stacey didn't need a second invitation. So off they went at a nod from Cathy and me, and disappeared into the trailer.

'The lodge isn't quite ready yet,' said Georgia. 'Why don't you come inside and wait?'

We followed Georgia up the steps. At the top lay a husky that looked like a cuddly bear. There were also puppies running around, excited by the welcome interruption to their routine.

On the inside the trailer looked a lot bigger than on the outside. We were introduced to Nina, who was slightly older than Georgia but very similar in looks. We had brought some tobacco and red cloth as an offering. Cathy gave them to Nina, who was going to the lodge to prepare it for the sweat.

Sweating is one of many ceremonies that are common to Native American tribes, varying only in detail. The lodge is like a sauna, and water is poured over hot stones to create cleansing steam.

'Tony,' said Georgia, 'you and Craig can come and help me pick some white sage. We need quite a lot for the sweat.'

Cathy remained in the trailer with Nina and Georgia's mother, who lived in a cabin-style house next to the home of her daughters. Nina showed her some of the quilts her mother made—beautiful and spectacular things, decorated with wolf and buffalo designs.

After we'd collected the sage, Georgia, Craig and I took the bundles to the lodge, which was a wooden, arched frame covered by canvas and blankets. A buffalo skull was placed at the entrance.

Nina was there already, with Cathy, and was shovelling hot sandstones from a large pit that stood close by. The stones are heated for hours in the pit and then placed into a smaller pit inside the lodge.

Objects needed for the sweat were placed just outside the entrance. Beside the tobacco and red cloth we had brought were a pipe and a crystal stone.

'Dad, Mum's got to take all her clothes off,' said Craig.

'What?' I said. 'She's going in naked?'

'I don't know,' said Craig, highly amused by the whole business, 'but she's looking embarrassed.'

Then Cathy appeared. She wasn't naked, but wore a very long and old T-shirt that had lots of holes in it. She looked for all the world like a war-torn refugee.

'Craig said you were going in naked,' I said, winking at my son. Cathy said nothing, but gave me one of those 'what have you got me into now?' sort of looks.

Nina had overheard Craig's and my conversation. 'Yes,' she said, 'women do usually go in naked, but because you and the boys are going in we'll be wearing something.'

'Oh,' was all I could think of to say, glad to be relieved of any possibility of embarrassment.

'By the way,' said Nina, 'rings or any other metal you're wearing will have to be taken off. They'll get so hot in there they'll burn you.'

Once the stones were inside the lodge, the heat from them could be felt even outside. I began to wonder what the heat would be like on the *inside*. My chance to find out came, as we were invited to step inside, from the left-hand side, on our hands and knees. We had been instructed to say—as a mark of respect to our ancestors —'All our relatives' as we entered. It had also been explained to us that there would be three sittings and the lodge would therefore be opened twice during the ceremony. This would allow those who felt a little overcooked to get out into the cooler air.

Eight of us were taking part: my family and I, and Georgia, Nina and Sky. Once inside the lodge, we noticed that the sage we'd picked was scattered on the floor. There were blankets on the floor, too, for us to sit on, and hanging on the frame of the lodge was a piece of red cloth, some sage and a buffalo skull.

We sat in a circle around the pit. Georgia closed the entrance and the room went black as night—and very hot very quickly.

'Mammy, I don't like it,' Stacey moaned pitifully from the opposite side to me. Georgia asked her, 'Do you want to go out, Stacey?'

'Yes.'

So the entrance was opened and Stacey crawled out—much faster than she had crawled in.

'If any of you get too hot,' said Nina, 'lie on the floor. It's a little cooler there.'

The entrance was then closed once more. Within minutes the boys were lying down. Nina was praying and giving thanks to the gods and the spirits of her ancestors. In the blackness, sweating profusely, hearing Nina's soft-spoken words of prayer in her own. tongue, I found my mind wandering back to the reason we were here: our Madoc–Mandan link. It was only the offer of a drink of water from a buffalo horn that brought me round. I don't know how long I'd sat, sedated by the hypnotic quality of my surroundings.

'Tony,' said Nina. 'Take this. Put some on your head, on your eyes, on all your body if you want to. And drink some. What you don't use, throw on the stones.'

I did as Nina told me. Even though the water had become warm in the stiflingly hot atmosphere, it nevertheless seemed cool and refreshing by comparison. As I threw the water on the stones, the heat rose dramatically, and the room seemed even hotter.

Eventually, it was time to open the entrance for the

first time. Cathy, the boys and I were keen to get some cool air into our lungs. Outside the sun seemed a thousand times brighter than it had before we'd gone in. The breeze was cooling and very welcome, and we drank thirstily from bottled water we'd brought with us. Cathy's torn T-shirt was clinging to her body, wet with sweat.

We were one down for the second sitting: Sky had decided she didn't want to go back in. She wanted to remain outside and play with Stacey.

During the sweating we took turns to give thanks for our newfound friends, and asked for strength to be given to any family or friends who might be ill or suffering.

The sweat-lodge, inside and out.

Georgia and Nina then offered more prayers, both in English and their native language.

During the third sitting the pipe was lit. Now I'm not the fanciful type when it comes to visions and things, but—and I'm not sure whether this was the effect of the heat, the smoke from the pipe or both—I swear I saw the head of a wolf. Matthew hadn't used the pipe, but swore he'd seen a fish.

After the third session we once again crawled out into the welcoming cool air, feeling light and relaxed. Back at the trailer we were entertained to a buffet of sliced meats, bread rolls, crisps—or potato chips, as our hosts call them—cheese and various other tasty titbits. All that sweating had given us an appetite.

After we'd eaten, Georgia announced, 'I've got something for you all.' She disappeared into her bedroom and emerged with some feathers. She handed a large one each to Cathy and me, and some smaller ones to the children.

'They're eagle feathers,' she explained. 'They're held by the tribe to be sacred symbols, and it's considered an honour to be given them. An honour not bestowed on many whites,' she added.

The time had come for us to take our leave once more of the Fort Berthold reservation and its people. We were sorry to say goodbye, but not sorry the filming was over.

I suspected that the natives weren't too sorry, either. Alan could be a bit overbearing, and I don't think he endeared himself to them. To them there was nothing below the surface persona of a very English man with a very English accent, who seemed constantly to have a cigar on the go. The cigar seemed like some sort of comforter, and he certainly didn't seem as at ease when he *didn't* have one lit.

Before we left we did some shopping at the mall in Minot. The children had lists of friends and teachers they wanted to take gifts to. Matthew's teacher, Mr Sanders, has himself travelled through Dakota—South, though, not the North—and was keen for Matthew to share his experiences with the class.

Craig, whose GCSE exams were getting closer, felt he had done enough globetrotting for the time being. He always took a pile of books with him on our travels, but he was keen now to get back to studying in a more conventional way—in a school. There would be plenty of life for travelling.

I was happy that my family had shared my experiences—both of the Cook Islands as the 'Swiss Family Williams', and here in North Dakota, among the Mandans.

Soon we were driving away from Fort Berthold, and I realized that I was the only one awake, which was just as well because I was at the wheel. Our stay here was at an end, but that of our friend Harry Sitting Bear to Wales was about to begin. He had been asked by tribal elders to join me in pursuit of the Madoc–Mandan link.

Chapter Nineteen

The Celts and the quiche

August 1996. We're all at Wales Airport, Cardiff, awaiting the arrival of Harry Sitting Bear. Cathy, Matthew, Stacey and Cathy's cousin Paul decided to come along and be part of the welcoming committee.

He was an impressive sight as he came towards us in the concourse—a powerfully built man with distinctive features. We introduced him to Paul and then decided to take him to his hotel for much-needed rest.

'On my way here,' said Harry in the car, 'a woman asked me if I was going to a powwow. "No," I told her, "I'm going to put the English on reservations." She didn't know if I was joking.'

Alan's film company was paying for Harry's stay. He'd been booked into the Marriot Hotel in Swansea.

'You'll be wanting to rest up a little before we show you any sights,' Cathy suggested as we helped him into his room with his luggage.

'Just one thing first,' he said. With a flourish he unrolled a magnificent buffalo robe and spread it on the bed. It was quite spectacular, hand-painted with colourful symbols representing his people and their ways and culture. It must have meant something to Harry to want to show us this before resting after a tiring journey.

Early that evening I collected Harry from his hotel. He had rested well and was ready to let us take him off to meet people. First stop was Paul's house in a quiet cul-desac. Paul and his wife Hilda met us on the doorstep, and Harry seemed to take to Hilda immediately, remarking on how attractive her Scottish lilt sounded to his American ears.

As we strolled through their garden, which was sporting a variety of flowers and shrubs, Harry complimented Paul on how beautiful the garden looked, but Paul said it was all down to Hilda.

'She's known locally as the flower doctor,' he said. 'People bring her their dying plants and she brings them back to life.'

'Flowers know when they're with a caring person,' said Harry.

Another thing he liked about her was her cooking— and he demanded her quiche recipe to take back to North Dakota with him.

After our meal we drove to Bwlch and looked out over the Rhondda Valley. Surrounded with lush forestry, we wanted to give Harry a short taste of our own land. Paul explained how the coal-mining industry had diminished, how once it had been a major source of work for the Valleys folk, it was now very much in decline.

Harry sympathized, saying that the flooding of the lusher and more productive parts of his reservation had robbed many of his own people of their livelihoods, forcing them to eke out a living in other ways.

Paul, Hilda, Cathy and I had done a recce before Harry arrived, to establish what were the best places to show him, and had drawn up an itinerary of sorts. The following day we took him first to Castell Henllys near Cardigan in West Wales. This is the site of a reconstructed Iron Age Celtic village.

It took us about an hour and a half to drive from Swansea to Cardigan. 'So much land,' Harry mused, as he gazed through the car window. 'Yet all the houses I see are very close together. Your sheep have more land than your people.'

We parked the car and walked up the narrow lane that leads the way to the site. Harry laughed as we turned a sharp bend and came face to face with a reconstructed hairy mammoth. Paul pretended to wrestle with it.

We were met by the site manager, Phil Bennett, who knew we were bringing a visitor from the Mandans' home in Dakota. Phil introduced us to Lester Mason, one of the seasonal site guides.

'Let's go into one of the houses,' Lester suggested. 'We can talk there.'

We went into the largest of the reconstructed houses. Harry said he could see some similarities with the earth lodges, yet houses like these had been used thousands of years ago. Like the earth lodges, they are round, and the people who lived in them had a central hearth. They were made of wattle and daub, with roof timbers covered with thatch of water reed.

We walked and talked and Lester gave us a tour of the grounds, stopping in front of a wooden sculpture carved out a piece of oak.

'What's this?' asked Harry.

Lester was only too keen to explain. 'This represents the hunter Mabon, from the Mabinogion.'

'The Mabi—?'

'Mabinogion,' said Lester, who went on to explain that the Mabinogion is a collection of eleven Welsh prose tales of the 11th to the 13th centuries. They deal with Celtic

Harry Sitting Bear at Castell Henllys iron-age fort, Pembrokeshire.

legends and mythology. (The word comes from the Welsh
'*Mabinogi*', meaning 'youth' or 'tale of youth' or
'instruction for young bards'.) These tales are to be found
in *The White Book of Rhydderch* (c. 1300–25), *The Red
Book of Hergest* (c. 1375–1425) and other manuscripts.

Although written, they're all largely based on earlier oral traditions describing mythology and heroism.

This particular sculpture had impressed Harry, we could see. It wasn't unlike a totem pole in some ways, although we couldn't claim a link here, because it was produced by a contemporary artist. In fact, it is part of a sculpture trail designed by the West Wales Artists' Group, each work representing an aspect of these folk tales that are so important to Celtic mythology. It depicted Mabon, known as 'the greatest hunter in the world', who, according to legend, was missing for a great number of years.

Lester went on to explain that, as with the American Indians, animals played an important part in Celtic stories. He showed us several animal carvings, again representing aspects of the Mabinogion. Harry asked us to take some photographs of them for him to take back to show his people.

Next stop was the Llysyfran Reservoir, a few miles away at Maenclochog, where we stopped to eat. There are stories about the Llysyfran reservoir, that it, like the Garrison Dam in North Dakota, flooded homes when the reservoir was created in the seventies. There are tales of bells heard in the night—but the people at the visitor centre there tell me these are just that: tales. There are no homes under the water.

Back at Paul's and Hilda's, Harry was keen to learn the secret of the quiche. Hilda explained that she baked from memory, and used her hands to measure the quantities of ingredients. Harry's hands are three times the size of Hilda's, so she promised to make another quiche and write down some quantities that would be safe for him to follow.

He would be taking home from Wales a recipe written out by a Scotswoman for a dish with a French name to introduce to his Mandan friends in the United States of America.

It's a funny old world.

Chapter Twenty

Messing about on the river

Tuesday, 13 August 1996, and it's time for filming.

The crew, too, had stayed at the Marriot, so we were able to travel in a small convoy back to west Wales. For this part of the shoot, we were booked into a picturesque, two-hundred-year-old hotel, the Castell Malgwyn, which sits in forty-eight acres of land very close to the River Teifi. We were back near Cardigan, this time in the charming village of Llechryd.

The hotel would make a good backdrop for some of our shots. The presence of the River Teifi was not just to make a pretty picture: this was where we were to illustrate another link between the Celts and the Mandans—the coracle. Like the Native American bull boats, the Welsh coracles—still in use—are made from willow. In earlier times, they, like the bull boats, were made of hide, but these days calico is used, and made waterproof with tar.

The crew set up their gear on a small bridge quite close to the hotel.

Our host for this part of the shooting was a sprightly seventy-four-year-old coracle-maker called Bernard Thomas, who was to be filmed on the river with Harry Sitting Bear. Harry didn't say anything, until he saw Bernard pull up in his car and remove the coracles from the back.

'I'm not going in that,' said Harry, half laughing. 'I'll turn it into a submarine.' Obviously he had never been in a bull boat either, since they're not used very much any more

'I'm sure it'll be fine,' Alan reassured him, glancing at Bernard for some sort of support.

'Yes, you'll be all right, my boy,' said Bernard in his pronounced Welsh accent. Harry seemed to relax a little, and did get into the coracle. Did I spot a mischievous gleam in Bernard's eye?

Soon they were adrift, both in identical coracles, having pushed themselves off gently from the riverside.

I can't vouch for the accuracy of the conversation, because I didn't know until afterwards what they'd been saying to each other, but as they floated down the Teifi Harry and Bernard talked of their love and respect for all things natural. Bernard, like Harry, had been close to the things that mattered: when you're making things with your hands, things that have been used for centuries, you do tend to feel grounded.

'I'm one of the last of the people making these,' Bernard told Harry. 'There's not many of us left now, boy. We're a dying breed, we are.'

'It's good that you do this,' said Harry. 'There's a lot of pleasure to be had from working with your hands, working with natural things.'

'This coracle once helped me to get a fish-hook out of a cygnet's neck,' Bernard told Harry. 'Mind you, the mother didn't like it. The hook got caught right in the side of the little one's neck, see. So off I went in my coracle, chasing the poor thing. It was frightened, I can tell you. The mother was interfering all the way. But then she wouldn't be a good mother if she didn't, would she?

She didn't understand what was going on, did she? So I eventually cornered the cygnet and took the hook out.'

Bernard told Harry of the mythical goddess of the Teifi. 'Supposed to take care of the river and all the fish that swim in it,' he said. 'There's a story here that once there are no more coracles on the river there'll be no more salmon. There's not many of us using the coracles now, see, and there's not much salmon left, either.'

Bernard had obviously impressed Harry. He told me later, 'You know, Tony, for a moment there, talking to Bernard, I felt at home, almost like I was back on the reservation.'

And soon he was sampling another bit of hospitality from Bernard—his home-made elderflower wine. After filming was done for the day and the interviews were in the can, Harry, Cathy and I went by invitation to Bernard's home, a small house that didn't look much higher than about seven feet. There was an anthracite fire, with a two-seater settee at either side. A half-made coracle was in the room with us.

Soon Bernard was refilling our glasses. Cathy refused, and Bernard made a joke about the wine and how it gave women hairs on their chests.

Harry broke into a chuckle as he examined the half-finished coracle in the corner.

Bernard Thomas is one of Wales's true characters. In spite of his age, he's out frequently on the river in his coracle, and even flies a microlight aeroplane, looking down on the village from several hundred feet above.

Even tonight, after several glasses of this rather potent wine, he'd be out on the Teifi in the dark, fishing for salmon in his coracle.

'Well, drive carefully, now, boy,' Bernard said to me as we were ready to take our leave. And to Cathy he said, 'And I'll be up to Castell Malgwyn later to check your chest for hairs.'

Harry was keen to see more coracles. Their similarity with the bull boats that were so familiar to him back home had excited his interest, and so, on the way back to our hotel, we called in to the coracle centre at Cenarth not far away from Llechryd. Here he soon made another friend, Martin, who showed us around the centre eagerly, obviously feeling quite honoured to have a genuine Native American hanging on his every word.

Martin joined us at the hotel later to see the spectacular buffalo robe Harry had shown us previously. As we walked in the pitch darkness around the hotel grounds that night, stopping for a chat on the tiny bridge we'd used earlier in the day, the world seemed so tranquil that it was hard to believe that men still fought over land. Cathy seemed quite moved by the stillness. 'You know, if Dylan Thomas was here,' she said, 'he would write a poem about it.'

And it was strange to reflect, too, that somewhere out there in the sloe-black, slow, black, fishingboat-bobbing night, Bernard was in his hand-crafted coracle, fishing for salmon, with or without the help of the goddess.

Early next morning we left Llechryd for north Wales—Anglesey. This was Madoc country—the former county of Gwynedd, which was the name of Madoc's father, Owain. It took us four and a half hours, passing through towns such as Aberystwyth, Dolgellau, Porthmadog, Caernarfon. The last of these—as we explained to Harry—was where the investiture of an *English* Prince of Wales took place in 1969!

The castle here is quite a landmark—built by Edward I in 1284, a hundred and fourteen years after Madoc's journey west. It's amusing that a castle originally intended to subjugate the Welsh should now be benefiting a great many people in Caernarfon and surrounding areas, since it attracts so many tourists during the summer months and is a significant help to the local economy.

After the very open plains of Dakota, Harry loved the scenery in mid and north Wales, the hills and mountains, the landscape carpeted in places with purple heather.

We crossed the Menai Bridge and made our way up to Beaumaris, where Cathy decided we ought to book Harry into his hotel before we went and did the same at the one opposite. There was a function here this evening in Harry's honour. We all wanted to be fresh for the occasion.

We went up with Harry in the old-fashioned lift, the type with the manual doors.

When Harry opened the door to his room, Cathy was aghast.

'What's this supposed to be?' she asked. 'It's pathetic.'

It was, indeed, very small for a big man. Harry's frame almost filled it.

'This is no good for you, Harry,' I said, feeling embarrassed, even though we'd had nothing to do with the hotel bookings.

Harry looked at the room for a while, peeked into the bathroom and said, 'Geez! The bathtub is bigger than the bed.'

'We'll get you another room,' said Cathy.

We decided to wait until the crew arrived. Then we'd have a chat with Alan. Meanwhile, Cathy and I went to our own hotel, where, compared with Harry's room, ours, with its four-poster bed, was luxury.

We learned that the four-hundred-year-old hotel was supposed to be haunted. The receptionist showed us one room that no maid would go into alone. In another, a guest had once woken to find a woman sitting on the bed looking down at him. In a third room, perfume bottles are said to be knocked off the dressing table by an unseen force, if the ghostly inhabitant doesn't like the smell.

'I think we'd better go and check on Harry,' said Cathy, as if she'd seen quite enough, thank you very much. I suppressed a chuckle. My normally level-headed wife was beginning to get worried about the ghosts.

We spotted him across the street. He'd been buying gifts for family and friends. We all looked around Beaumaris for a while and then decided we'd take a tour on one of the horse-drawn carts that are to be seen in this lovely little town. Beaumaris (which derives from the French and means 'beautiful marsh': *beau marais*) has another of Wales's English-built castles—again erected by Edward I to consolidate his conquest of north Wales in the thirteenth century.

As we neared our hotel, we saw Alan and Jill Dales, his assistant, pull up outside.

'I'll tell Jill to organize another room for you,' said Cathy to Harry.

Alan told us that the rest of the crew had stopped off at Porthmadog to see the tourist-attraction village of Portmeirion, which was the setting for the 1960s TV series, *The Prisoner*.

We learned that Jill couldn't manage another room for Harry—everywhere was booked. So she and he did a swap. I think she thought we were exaggerating until she saw the room for herself. But she fitted into it better than Harry ever would.

The function in honour of Harry Sitting Bear's visit to north Wales was at a gallery, Oriel Ynys Môn. Harry had taken along the buffalo robe.

Introductions were made in both English and Welsh, and singing and dancing had been planned, including some traditional Celtic dances in clogs, and some involving animal skins. This one was like musical chairs, except that it wasn't a chair that was removed from the proceedings but one of the female dancers. When the music stopped the males ran to join up with a female, but the one that missed out had to wear the skin over his head and would be laughed at and jeered by the others.

Harry seemed at home, and laughed freely at the comical dance taking place.

Harry had been seated next to the local council leader, Gareth Winston Roberts, who now went on to the stage to make the official welcome. He said he hoped our Native American guests had enjoyed his evening so far, and invited him up on to the stage. There he was presented with a framed print of some Welsh standing stones—of which there are many—and a tie with the council emblem on it.

During the refreshments interval, the talk was of Madoc. All those present—townsfolk, civic dignitaries, those interested in heritage and ethnicity—seemed interested in what we were trying to do, our attempt to prove the link between our Prince Madoc and Harry's ancestors, or at least prove that there was justification for reopening the debate.

The second half of the proceedings showed Harry another Welsh tradition: the playing of the harp. At the end of the evening, a local bard, Richard Jones, called Harry to the rostrum. Harry's resplendent buffalo robe had been pinned to a board behind him. After making a speech in which he welcomed Harry on behalf of the bards of Wales, Richard Jones presented him with a crystal bowl engraved with the poetic message:

> *Iwerydd o hen hiraeth—a gorchest*
> *Gwarchod hen dreftadaeth*
> *Ynom sydd, er blaenllym saeth*
> *Byd aliwn i'm bodolaeth.*
>
> Talybolion
(Richard Jones)

Which in English means:

> We are linked by an Atlantic of yearning and the achievement of protecting our heritage, despite an alien world's hostility to our existence.

The message was headed '*Cymru a'r Mandan*', Wales and the Mandan.

Harry, we could see, was moved. He made a short speech of acceptance, and had a special message for the elderly people at the ceremony. Old people, he said, had a very special position in the tribes. They were highly respected and treated with reverence.

'They are seen as the root from which we come,' he said. 'They are wise and knowledgeable, and should be held in high esteem.'

Harry Sitting Bear at Oriel Ynys Môn, his buffalo robe proudly displayed behind him.

He told the smiling audience that he felt very much at home in Wales, and sensed a strong link with the people and their language. He turned then to the buffalo robe behind him, and explained that each of the animals depicted there had a special significance for his people.

The event had been caught on film, of course, for Alan's documentary. I could hardly believe as we drove back into the centre of Beaumaris and to our hotel that our simple quest for the Madoc–Mandan link would have led to all this.

We made another early start. The previous evening, after the proceedings at Oriel Ynys Môn, we had all gone through our itinerary. Our destination was Llys Rhosyr in Newborough and in particular an archaeological site where the remains of Owain Gwynedd's palace are being unearthed. Of all the places in Wales that we'd taken Harry so far, this was the one that would bring him closest to his earliest ancestors.

Our convoy of cars arrived at the site, which was surrounded by security wire, within which I could make out various shapes of rooms. I felt a compelling urge to stand among those stones, imagine the walls around me as they were in the twelfth century when the young Madoc wandered from room to room thinking of ships and the sea and journeys to uncharted lands.

A further car pulled up behind our own vehicles and two men got out whom Alan immediately greeted. He brought them over to us.

'This is Harry Sitting Bear,' he said to them. 'And Tony and Cathy Williams, and Jill, my PA. This'—he indicated the newcomers to us—'is David Longley and Cecil Jones.' They were both archaeologists working on the dig.

Alan would be interviewing Cecil, David and Harry at the site, but before filming began we put to Cecil the question we seemed to have put to everyone we'd met over the past few weeks: did he believe in the link?

The remains of one of Owain Gwynedd's palaces, Llys Rhosyr.

'Yes, of course. And did you know that Madoc was part Viking?' he asked.

'Yes,' I answered. 'I did.' I remembered what I had read of Owain Gwynedd's grandfather, who had married a Viking, Princess of Dublin.

Well, then,' Cecil enthused, 'Madoc would have known about routes the Norse people took, because they would have discussed their travels with their Welsh relations.'

'So you're saying you think he went to America on a Viking ship?' I asked.

'That's very feasible. The Welsh and the Vikings had an alliance at the time.'

The site we were using as our backdrop was the first of its kind: a palace built for Welsh royalty. David Longley was intrigued to find someone so committed to the legend of Madoc. I asked David if I could have one of the stones from the site. Reluctantly, he acquiesced, and before he could change his mind I'd hauled one to the car, my knees bending with the weight.

Harry watched, laughing, as I feebly attempted to haul the thing into the boot, but I managed it, wincing in sympathy with my rear suspension as I watched the back of the car dip considerably.

Filming didn't go too well. The interview with the three men was mainly about the Vikings and their presence in Wales in the twelfth century. There were cuts and retakes. An hour passed. Harry finally walked away from the front of the camera and came over to Cathy and me.

'Tony, I want to go home,' he said.

Alan came rushing over to us.

'Is there anything wrong, Harry?' he asked.

'I've come over here to meet the people of Wales,' he said, 'not talk about Vikings.'

Alan promised him that the interview was almost over, and Harry continued. His perseverance was rewarded when discussion turned to the Welsh. And he felt more a part of things when Cecil asked him whether there was talk within the tribe about Madoc.

Harry told the two archaeologists about the similarities between the coracle and the bull boat. He reiterated his story of the Lone Man and a tale Louella had told us of the magic boat with its animal head.

He had got into his stride again, and seemed disappointed when Alan said he had all he needed. However, the filming wasn't quite over. Some establishing shots needed taking, some of them from a helicopter. One shoot was to be at some standing stones, and yet another would be of Harry standing on a cliff looking out to sea.

The stones were about half an hour's drive away. The crew assembled their gear as Harry, Cathy and I stood chatting. We were filmed facing them, pointing to them as though discussing them, as the helicopter hovered above us.

Time was getting on, and it was about five o'clock when we set off for the last shooting site. We were expected at the Pritchard Jones Hall in Newborough at 7 p.m. Another little gathering in Harry's honour had been arranged.

'We're not going to get there in time,' Cathy said, looking at her watch.

But Alan insisted. Schedules and all that. Had to be done.

So off we went and Cathy and I watched from our car as the helicopter hovered above Harry, who stood on the cliff top, looking out to sea, looking towards his home thousands of miles away.

When Harry arrived at our car he had a small posy of wild flowers and, handing them to Cathy, said, 'For a Welsh princess.'

We were late for the gathering. We'd have been their much earlier if we hadn't got back to our haunted hotel to find that our belongings had disappeared from our room. Odd goings on indeed—ghosts wanting to steal modern clothes.

We went to the reception desk to ask what had happened. There'd been a shift change and it wasn't the receptionist who had shown us round earlier. Someone who looked like he might be the manager stood next to her.

'We have a problem,' he explained. 'Your room was double booked.' He pointed to the corner of the small office, and there stood our luggage.

We declared that we'd never be staying there again, and left, finding that there was now a room available at Harry's hotel. The function wasn't as formal an affair as that of the previous evening. No civic dignitaries this time—but many ordinary Welsh citizens who wanted to meet Harry and talk to us about our quest. They had waited patiently a full hour beyond the start time.

Even so, there was a round of spirited applause as Harry walked into the room. The atmosphere was casual and relaxed. Harry was presented with a Welsh love spoon. He seemed quite moved and, when the time came for him to make a short speech, he said he had not expected the welcome and respect he'd been shown since he'd arrived in Wales.

'Where I come from, the natives aren't that well thought of,' he said. 'I come here and find I fit in easily, that people are warm.'

He told us how his people and their language almost met extinction, and he spoke of similarities between the histories of the Mandan and the Welsh peoples.

Everyone seemed to want to talk to him after that. He felt like a football star who'd given a kid an autograph, and found a hundred more clamouring for his signature. Except that, with Harry, it was a moment of two of conversation.

One elderly lady asked him, 'Why doesn't this happen any more, people gathering together and talking?' Why indeed? It was a rhetorical question, and Harry had no answer, any more than we did.

During the voracious partaking of ham, pickled onions, cheese, cakes, sandwiches and a hundred and one other things on the buffet in an adjoining room, Harry told stories of his people, and his grandfather in particular, and many offered their four penn'orth of comment on the Madoc–Mandan link.

'Did you know Welsh sailors were all blond-haired and blue-eyed?' one chap asked. Another said, 'The Druids were like the Native Americans: they worshipped the sun and the earth.'

Soon—too soon—it was past eleven o'clock. The evening had to draw to a close. So soon would Harry's stay in Wales. He had done what he'd come here for: had spoken to those people who I believe share an ancestry with him; he had taken part in Alan Ereira's documentary; he had seen for himself the land of his fathers.

Harry, Cathy and I made an early start back to Swansea. We left Alan and his crew behind. We stopped off at Dolgellau so Harry could pick some mountain heather for Paul's wife, Hilda, so she could add some to her already lush garden.

We spent our last evening together in Clyne Gardens in Swansea. Here are fifty acres of parkland, full of trees, shrubs, bushes of several varieties. We sat on a bench by a stream and Harry tapped out a rhythm on a small drum and sang native songs. Stacey and Matthew were with us—Hilda and Paul, too. All of us were moved by Harry's singing.

If you'd told me a year before that I'd be sitting in the middle of Wales's second city, listening to an American Indian playing a drum and singing I'd have thought you mad.

A lot seemed to have happened in such a short time. Our longed-for trip to North Dakota, the fortuitous accident that had put my embryonic typescript into the hands of a film-maker, the recce, the filming: it had been an eventful time for the whole family.

And if this book has done only one thing I'll be happy. If it's opened up the debate once more, brought more people into the argument over Madoc—people who might never have really thought about the link until now—then I'll have achieved something.

As I said at the outset, I'm neither a historian nor an anthropologist. But, then, I don't believe in leaving everything to the experts, either. I've met many people along the way who believe in the Madoc-Mandan link, and I'm sure I'll meet many more. Even if the 'experts' come down, once again, against such a link, I'm sure there will always be a nagging doubt at the backs of most people's minds.

At the end of the day, how can anybody really *know*?

We saw Harry off at the airport. It seemed as if he'd arrived only that morning, instead of several days ago. He had to take one suitcase more than he'd arrived with, to accommodate all the gifts that had been showered upon him. Cathy and I had given him a plaque engraved with a Welsh poem. Paul and Hilda had given him a clock depicting an eagle.

I was the last of us to hug this bear of a man, and when I pulled back my head and looked at his eyes I saw tears.

''Bye, Harry,' we all shouted in unison as Harry Sitting Bear disappeared through the gate towards his flight back to that *other* land of his fathers.

Acknowledgements

My thanks are due to Harry Sittingbear, Ed Lone Flight, Doris McGrady and Luther Grinnell who welcomed us to their reservation and helped us a great deal with our quest; to Georgia and Nina Fox, Katy Youngbear and her mother Louella, Edwin Benson and all the other friends, especially the elders, on the reservation who shared with us their wonderful culture; to Paul and Hilda Taylor for their support.